# THE
# LIGHTHOUSE OF TRUTH

*To Basia,
Keep Searching for the Truth,
Pax Vobiscum.
Bobbie
(Elizabeth Raikes)*

# THE
# LIGHTHOUSE OF TRUTH

by

ELIZABETH RAIKES

Regency Press (London & New York) Ltd.
125 High Holborn, London WC1V 6QA.

Copyright © 1994 by Elizabeth Raikes

This book is copyrighted under the Berne Convention. No portion may be reproduced by any process without the copyright holder's written permission except for the purposes of reviewing or criticism, as permitted under the Copyright Act of 1956.

ISBN 0 7212 0814 2

Printed and bound in Great Britain by
Buckland Press Ltd., Dover, Kent.

*Dedicated to*

**BROTHER JOHN**

and

our healers, inspirers, teachers and friends on the unseen side of life.

# ACKNOWLEDGEMENTS

I would like to thank Shiela Danton and the Winterbourne Writers' Group for their constructive criticism of my writing, introducing me to and rescuing me from the intricacies of the word processor and teaching me the do's and dont's of the world of publishing.

I greatly appreciate the time given up by my friends and patients who have written their stories for me and the many others who have shown interest in the project.

Also my thanks are due to my husband for his support and encouragement from day one of this lengthy enterprise.

## CONTENTS

| | Page |
|---|---|
| Acknowledgements | 6 |
| Preface | 9 |
| Introduction | 10 |

*Chapter*

| | |
|---|---|
| One | 11 |
| Two | 14 |
| Three | 17 |
| Four | 20 |
| Five | 24 |
| Six | 28 |
| Seven | 30 |
| Eight | 33 |
| Nine | 37 |
| Ten | 42 |
| Eleven | 45 |
| Twelve | 49 |
| Thirteen | 52 |
| Fourteen | 54 |
| Fifteen | 59 |
| Sixteen | 64 |
| Seventeen | 68 |
| Eighteen | 71 |
| Nineteen | 76 |
| Twenty | 79 |
| Twenty-one | 83 |
| Twenty-two | 86 |
| Twenty-three | 90 |
| Twenty-four | 94 |
| Twenty-five | 99 |
| Twenty-six | 103 |
| Twenty-seven | 105 |
| Twenty-eight | 111 |
| Bibliography | 114 |
| Useful Addresses | 116 |

## LIST OF ILLUSTRATIONS

| | | |
|---|---|---|
| One | Laurie. | 21 |
| Two | 'Truus'. | 42 |
| Three | Psychic drawing of Dr. Charles Henrie Monet du Salvan. | 73 |
| Four | Kirlian Photography. | 89 |
| Five | Sri Sathya Sai Baba. | 95 |
| Six | Darshan at Brindavan (Whitefields). Sai Baba surrounded by his devotees. | 101 |
| Seven | Sudha and Rani. | 108 |
| Eight | Mike and the author with the car. | 112 |

## PREFACE

Are you afraid of dying? Do you wonder what will happen to 'you', when the inevitable transition occurs?

Have you found no solace in the teachings of the orthodox religions?

Are you inwardly convinced that there is a deeper meaning to life which has nothing to do with 'going to church'?

Do you ask the question "Why am I here?"

If you have answered "Yes" to the above questions then read on. You may find a philosophy which will open up a new pathway of thought for you. You may discover the real purpose for your life.

Have you always treated Spiritualists, Mediums and Healers with lively suspicion?

Have you been shattered to the depths of your being by the loss of a loved one?

Have members of the medical profession said that you must 'live with' your painful condition?

Do you think contact with those who have 'died' is impossible? Would you like to be convinced otherwise?

Within these pages you will find evidence to support the case for 'life after death'. You will discover that mediums and healers are ordinary people who have developed special God-given talents to help their fellow men and women at times of distress in their lives. Practical advice and answers to many of your problems will be given and especially to the question which so many of us cry out at some time in our lives, "Why me?"

To prevent confusion and constant repetition of he/she I shall throughout the text refer to mediums, healers and patients as 'she'. No sexism is intended-this is merely for clarity and ease of reading.

## INTRODUCTION

"I am being told that you are writing. You have been thinking about this writing for a long time, but you have now begun and I have to tell you that it will be published."

Those astonishing few words were spoken to me on 1st March, 1991, by a complete stranger. At that time only Mike, my husband and my step-daughter Angela knew that six weeks previously I had picked up my pen in an attempt to express on paper ideas which had been going round in my mind for several years.

I was sitting in a large hall in the headquarters of the Spiritualist Association of Great Britain, in Belgrave Square, London. Mike and I had just walked in off the street to rest our aching feet after pounding the pavements all day. We were two unknown people amongst about twenty strangers. The lady who singled me out was a Medium. Until that afternoon I did not know of her existence.

I quickly realized that my friends and helpers in the spirit world, at whose suggestion I had begun the writing, were taking the opportunity to provide encouragement when I least expected it. The book which you are now holding is proof that the information relayed to me that day was indeed correct.

This is an account of the search for Truth which my husband and I have been engaged in over the past sixteen years. It tells the story of how I gradually changed from atheist to a complete believer in God and the reality of the world of the Spirit.

During that time several mediums have told me that I am building a Spiritual Lighthouse. Through this writing I hope the beam from my Lighthouse will bring hope, enlightenment, understanding and Truth into many dark and lonely corners of our world.

My aim is to dispel any fear of death by demonstrating that 'life' is an on-going process. That which we refer to as 'death' is in fact a rebirth into life in a different dimension.

I hope to be able to demonstrate that there is a reason behind all our suffering, whatever form it takes, and to offer a signpost for those who wish to seek out their own Truth.

## CHAPTER ONE

"Tell her we'll meet her there on Sunday night."

When I said those few words to Mike, my husband, one evening in November, 1977, I could never have imagined the far reaching effect they would have on our lives and the lives of many others, too.

Over the previous months Mike had said to me on several occasions, "A colleague in the office keeps telling me we should go to a certain Spiritualist Church".

At that time I was an atheist and the mere word 'church' was enough for me to dismiss the suggestion completely. However, eventually I agreed to go along, for the sake of a quiet life as much as anything.

I had known about Spiritualism since my childhood, but never associated it with church-going. Our next-door neighbours in Gillingham, Kent, where I grew up were Spiritualists, and held regular meetings in their front room, much to the amusement of my brother and myself. In fact we would sometimes give a knock on the adjoining wall and think it was hilarious. Such is the ignorance of youth.

So I had no idea what to expect from a church devoted to Spiritualism.

We walked into a brightly lit hall, with a rostrum banked with flowers at the far end. There was a friendly buzz of conversation from the crowded rows of the congregation and we were cheerfully greeted at the door by the church President. An organist was playing gentle, non religious background music as we made our way to seats two rows from the front.

I looked around and was surprised to see a beautiful drawing of what I assumed to be the head of Christ. I know now that this was a symbol of spiritual power from a highly evolved soul. It was not there to be worshipped in any way.

On the dot of 6.30 p.m. the President of the church walked onto the rostrum followed by a gentlemen. She introduced him to the congregation as Mr. Morgan from Wales.

The service began with a hymn. The tune was well known but the words were unfamiliar. This was followed by prayers and an address by the gentleman on the platform. What remains with me today of Mr. Morgan's work that evening is the shock I received when his opening words were, "I can assure you all of one thing only, you are all going to die! It may be tomorrow, next year or in thirty years time, but it is going to happen one day." He paused and went on, "If it happens in the next ten minutes come back and tell us what it's like over there."

A ripple of laughter ran through the congregation, but for me this was something entirely new. People were openly talking about dying and even laughing about it. Someone was actually asking if we knew what happens to us when we die.

During my early years I had done a great deal of church-going, both Church of England and Non-Conformist. It was part of the social structure in those days, and one certainly didn't question the reason for going. However I don't recall hearing anyone mention actually dying, or living for that matter, and there certainly wasn't any laughter. All I remember is a ritual of prayers and responses read from a prayer book, which had been written in a by-gone age. There was a never-ending sermon based on a biblical text, which had no relevance whatsoever to my life here in the Twentieth Century. One was supposed to have this elusive commodity 'faith' in something one could neither see, hear or understand.

Even when quite young I felt that prayer should be something you feel inside and not words chanted in unison from a prayer book written by someone else.

That evening, in a small Spiritualist Church I felt everything said had a meaning for my life and the lives of every other human being.

It became apparent later, after another hymn, that Mr. Morgan was a medium. He stood up and began speaking to individual members of the congregation. He told them facts from their loved ones who were 'dead'. He gave information which he could not possibly have known without being in touch with the departed souls themselves. I now know that in Spiritualist circles this is called giving evidence of the continuity of life.

After all these years and many hundreds of meetings later I do not remember the exact details given on that particular evening. Suffice to say, Mike and I walked out of the church quite stunned. I recall saying to him as we walked back to the car, "That is the first time in my life I have ever been to a church service and actually listened and been interested in what was being said."

From that day Mike and I began investigating spirit communication with zealous enthusiasm. We visited every Spiritualist Church for miles around. When away on holiday we did not look to see what entertainments were available, we enquired the location of the nearest Spiritualist meeting. Our search led us to small back rooms, basements, purpose built churches, large halls and theatres. Anywhere there was a meeting, we would be in the audience.

Of course we accept now that this did not happen by chance. It was not luck that there was an exceptionally gifted medium on the platform on our first introduction to the wonders of spirit communication. The spirit world had arranged it all in order to get us launched on the work we had come back to earth to accomplish.

I am sure that many people who read those words will be unable to 'take on board' the underlying meaning of that last sentence. The idea that there are unseen influences in our lives will be wholly unacceptable. However, I can assure everyone that, when it was happening to me, I too would have been unable to accept that statement. We do not change the pattern of our thinking over night. It is a very gradual process. Eventually this new concept becomes an integral part of ones life.

So, to those for whom this is a new idea I say, "Do not dismiss these matters out of hand. Have an open mind and really study the facts. Make your own investigations. Before long you too will take for granted the evidence of spiritual influences in our lives."

After a while, Mike and I began to realize that not only could one be put in touch with departed loved ones through the Spiritualist Church, but there was a whole new philosophy waiting to be explored. A philosophy giving an entirely new meaning to life and death.

## CHAPTER TWO

When William Shakespeare wrote, "All the worlds a stage, And all the men and women merely players", he demonstrated that he had a deep knowledge of the philosophy which I have discovered and am about to discuss with you.

Yes, we are all here to play a specific role for an allotted amount of time. It may be just a few hours or it could be for a century. However long it is, you may be sure, it is all part of a divine plan.

When one starts out on this road to philosophical discovery there are many aspects which just cannot be accepted. However, as soon as one small idea has been understood and absorbed into the consciousness, the mind begins viewing everything from a different angle. A whole jigsaw puzzle of facts will gradually become a believable and acceptable picture. From small beginnings it is possible to build up a new philosophy of life.

The most difficult concept to understand when one sets out on this new pathway of thought is the fact that we are not physical bodies with a spirit. Exactly the opposite in fact. We are all spirit, who happen at this time to be clothed by our present bodies. Our spirit has inhabited many earthly bodies in the past and has played many different roles. It will play many others in the future. Life is eternal, and the physical body with which we are concerned at the present time is only a miniscule part of our whole lives. Life is endless. Nothing 'dies'.

Once a person is able to accept that underlying principle and alter their thinking accordingly, everything else will appear logical and begin to fall into place.

As I understand it, the world of the spirit vibrates much faster than our world of matter. Therefore, in order to survive earthly conditions the spirit must be clothed by a body vibrating at the same speed as matter. An astronaut going into space must wear a space suit in order to cope with the different conditions he will encounter when he leaves the earth's atmosphere. Our physical bodies are our space suits for living on earth.

A silver cord connects the two bodies. This is broken at death allowing the spirit to return to its rightful home. The old physical body is left behind like a worn out overcoat. Don't upset yourselves by weeping over graves and coffins. Your loved ones are not there. They are happy and free from pain in the world where they belong. The world where they will be waiting for you to join them, in the fullness of time.

"What is my Spirit?" is the question you're probably asking now.

When you speak about yourself and say 'I', to what are you referring? Is it your nose, your big toe, or even your brain? No, of course not, you know it is nothing physical. You are trying to define the indefinable. Your spirit, or your soul, is that part of you which makes you uniquely different from everyone else in the universe. It cannot 'die'.

Your next question will probably be, "Why do we come into life anyway, what is the purpose of it all?" A good searching question which I shall do my best to answer as simply as possible.

Every soul is striving for perfection, so that we may progress upwards in the spirit realms. There are many lessons which must be learned in order to purify the soul and some of those lessons can only be learned through human life with all its problems and suffering. Before each incarnation, with the help of more highly evolved souls than ourselves we decide on the conditions into which we need to be born in order that we might learn these lessons. A blueprint for our lives is drawn up so that the desired progress may be achieved. However, we are also given free will. It is up to each individual whether they listen to their consciences or not.

'Life' is like crossing the Atlantic on the QE2. Everyone is travelling to New York and there are dozens of ways of passing the time. If you choose to fritter away the whole journey betting in the Casino in a drunken haze, instead of listening to an interesting lecture or playing sport, you will have gained nothing from your experience. You will eventually reach the end of your journey and have to take stock of your behaviour.

All life is governed by Karma. That is a word used in Eastern religions and we would know it as the Law of Cause and Effect. This law is absolute throughout the Universe. Everything has an opposite in order to create balance.

When this concept is applied to our lives we could say, for instance, that if we did not experience sadness, how could we know the meaning of joy? If there was no darkness, how could we fully appreciate the sunlight?

There is a fine balance throughout the whole of our natural environment. Sensitive people are becoming very worried about the effect which industrialisation and the use of chemicals is having on our planet. The natural balance is being destroyed and the disasters which keep occurring are natures way of rectifying the situation. So it is with our lives. Everything, good or bad, must be evened out.

When we are deciding the circumstances of our next incarnation, one of the most important considerations is the working through of Karmic debts incurred in previous lives.

For instance, someone who was in a powerful position in an earlier life may have done nothing to improve the conditions of those under him. Next time round he would be on the receiving end of the suffering.

A person stricken with an illness in this life may have been in a position to help others several incarnations previously, but did nothing to alleviate the suffering. It may have taken several lifetimes before the right conditions could be arranged for the balancing of this Karmic debt. I feel quite sure that the more spiritually evolved we are the harder the conditions are that we are born into.

Grieving relatives searching for answers when an infant is a victim of what we call 'cot death', say, "Why should this innocent child, who has never harmed anyone, just die"?

First of all, what has to be realized and accepted is that the child is not dead. They have just returned to the world of Spirit, from whence they came, and really belong. Perhaps the child only incarnated because the parents had a very deep lesson to learn from their loss. The infant was blameless but part of its parents Karmic debt incurred in this life or a previous life.

When Mike and I try to explain Karma to those who are searching for answers to their deep questions about life, we use the following analogy.

'Life' is like going into a supermarket. The shelves are stacked with goodies and you are free to take whatever you wish and put it in your trolley. When you get to the checkout it must all be paid for. The same applies to our lives. Everything must be paid for, even if, for the time being, we put it on our credit card.

Of course not all Karmic debts are bad. Mike and I have been told that our healing gift is as a result of good Karma in previous lives.

Spiritual progress is made during the hard and difficult times through which we live. It is like the tempering of steel. The metal is no good until it has been put through fire and strengthened. Our characters become stronger as we battle against the metaphorical fires of life. The manner in which we handle the difficulties put before us is an indication of our spirituality.

Look back into your own life at a particularly painful period, when you suffered a great deal, either mentally, physically or both. Are you able to say, "Yes, I did become more patient, tolerant, understanding, sensitive to the feelings of others", or whatever description may apply in your case, as a result of that incident? If you are able to identify changes within yourself, then you are beginning to understand a little of what I am trying to explain.

## CHAPTER THREE

I realise that many people are quite unable to accept a philosophy which involves reincarnation. To me, it is the only logical explanation why we are all so different and playing such a variety of roles.

Think of Mother Theresa of Calcutta for example. Is it really possible for such a beautiful, loving, selfless individual to become as she is during just one lifetime? As I see it, she has evolved into that incredible human being through numerous incarnations, across many centuries of learning life's lessons.

We usually refer to a person who has this obvious inner spirituality as 'an old soul'. By this we mean someone who has lived many lifetimes and learned all the necessary lessons. Spirituality just shines out of them. They have reincarnated for a special mission to do good on this planet.

One of the best examples of an 'old soul' who crossed my path was a delightful, sensitive little boy of seven whom I met in the course of my work as a teacher of children with special needs. He was born into a very rough family and had a hearing problem. One day he said to me, "Do you know, I love everybody – I even love beetles!" What greater love can anyone aspire to than that? If a few more people in our world could say those words and mean them, what a different place it would be.

Looking back into history there are many famous souls whom, I believe, incarnated to perform a specific task. Winston Churchill is a fine example of this.

During the South African war he was taken prisoner by the Boers. He escaped and there was a price on his head. While looking for somewhere to hide from his pursuers he knocked on a door and asked for help. The occupants of that house were the only people for twenty miles around who were sympathetic to the British cause. Sceptics would say it was chance that led him to that specific house. I would say he was led there by unseen forces because he had other, far more important work to do forty years later. When he went to Buckingham Palace in 1940 to take over the role of wartime Prime Minister he said, "I felt I walked with Destiny." Deep within himself he knew that he had incarnated to do this important job. All his previous experience in this, and other lives, had been a preparation for the task he was about to undertake.

All human life is a progression and it seems to me that when something needs changing someone with the appropriate skills incarnates.

Florence Nightingale overcame what would have appeared to another soul insurmountable problems, in order to lay the foundations of our present nursing care in hospitals.

Abraham Lincoln was around when it was necessary to abolish slavery.

Consider the life of Mikhail Gorbachev. He, despite incredible opposition, changed the face of Soviet politics. The lives of millions of East Europeans have altered, we hope, for the better.

The vast majority of us have no memory of our previous lives. Some people have been regressed through hypnosis into other personalities which were supposedly themselves. I remain to be convinced on this subject. Having had no personal experience I would not dream of making any judgement either way.

However a number of people have total recall of a previous life.

A gentleman named E. W. Ryall remembered a life which he led in Somerset in the 17th Century. In his book, *Second Time Around*, he describes how all through his present life in Essex he knew about this other life even though he had never been to Somerset. He clearly remembered being run through with a pike and killed at the Battle of Sedgemoor. His book is well worth reading.

Another gentleman, the late Captain Flowerdew, had flashes of memory throughout his childhood of life as a soldier in a place made of pink and black stone. Many years later he saw a television programme about Petra in Jordan and recognised it as the place which he remembered. When he eventually visited Petra he was able to show his companions the exact spot where he had died at the age of thirty, two thousand years before. He was able to recall the day to day life of a soldier in that city hewn from the pink and black rock. The only building he was unable to recall was a huge Roman amphitheatre, but that was to be expected, because it had not been constructed till many years after his 'death' in that life.

George Patton, the famous American General of the Second World War, clearly remembered the place in North Africa where he had commanded a Carthaginian army against the Romans before the Christian era. He also recalled being with Napoleon at the retreat from Moscow.

These are just a few examples but there are many, many more.

Speaking personally, the more I think about actually 'living', the more miraculous it becomes. As the famous French philosopher Voltaire put it over two hundred years ago, "There is nothing more remarkable about being born twice than being born once." When you really think about it, all life is remarkable.

However, there has to be a reason for life and why some of us suffer more than others. As I look back over half a century I can see clearly the reason for all the hurt and pain which I had to undergo. Perhaps some of you may find parallels in your own lives and be able to answer some of your own questions regarding experiences through which you have had to struggle. There has to be a reason why I am writing this book. Perhaps it is to help you see your life in a different perspective.

If you are living through a particularly distressing time at the moment, try to stand back from the situation for just a short while. Look at the problem through different eyes. See it in the context of your whole life, which is Eternity.

A great spiritual philosopher named Silver Birch says, "Never judge a man till you have walked a mile in his moccasins."

In other words we cannot know what makes an individual behave in a certain manner, because we have not been through their suffering.

Attempt to work out a different way to react, when the next upsetting episode occurs. Our reactions influence the outcome of problems. Once again the Law of Cause and Effect comes into operation.

This is not an easy exercise, but learning situations never are.

## CHAPTER FOUR

Life in this incarnation began for me in September, 1930. I was born in Gillingham, Kent, the much loved youngest child with two older brothers. My parents were devoted to each other and their children.

Tragedy struck when I was four years old. My mother died, leaving my father to care for three children under the age of eleven.

I have no recollection of my mother, and as a child I always felt 'different' from other children, because I had no mother to whom I could refer. I remember saying in self defence, "My mother isn't really dead, her soul is still alive." I can't imagine anyone told me this, and I now assume that I brought the knowledge of 'life after death' back with me, when I came into 'life'.

All this happened before the days of the Welfare State which provides home helps and school dinners. However, 'Dad' would not hear of his family being broken up and we all lived happily with the help of a number of live-in housekeepers.

Everything was fine until the outbreak of war in 1939. My father took Laurie, the younger of my two brothers and myself to stay with my mother's sister in the heart of the Devonshire countryside. There were no other children for miles around, and nothing much to play with, as far as I can remember. Consequently, Laurie and I were much closer than a brother and sister would be under normal family circumstances. We were with our Aunt for about nine months and then Dad sent for us and we returned to Kent.

During our separation our father had remarried and moved from our home into his new wife's house. Our home and all its memories had gone for ever.

The Battle of Britain was just beginning and the next four months of our lives were spent diving in and out of the air raid shelter in the back garden. When we weren't in the shelter we were gazing up at the 'dogfights' overhead between Spitfires and Messerschmitts. It was a glorious summer that year of 1940 and the clear blue sky would be a mass of vapour trails from dozens of aircraft. My tenth birthday was spent in the garden counting the number of aircraft being shot down. No one gave any thought to the blowing out of cake candles in those perilous times.

By the end of September life became so dangerous in our area that my father took me to stay with relatives in the Gloucestershire countryside. The journey there was long and hazardous, since many of the railway lines had been blown up the night before. Everyone was trying to get away to places of safety and I can still remember the chaos of that journey. For the next two years I lived happily with my Aunt and Uncle before returning to Kent to live with my father and his wife.

*'Laurie' aged twenty-one years – forever young in my memory.*

This was the beginning of six years utter misery for me. My father's wife turned out to be a thoroughly domineering, bitter, nasty woman. My teenage years were a round of going to school, doing homework and working for my stepmother. My father allowed her to rule the roost. She was not an educated woman and when I was not doing her work I was expected to be knitting. In her opinion, reading was a waste of time. Strangely enough it was considered a great sin to either knit or sew on a Sunday, even though to my knowledge she never set foot inside a church.

My eldest brother had left home when my father remarried and Laurie joined the R.A.F. as soon as he was old enough. Thus, I was left to endure the vindictiveness of that dreadful woman on my own. Throughout my adolescent years I was treated as a child and a skivvy. Once again I felt different from all my school friends because I knew their lives were so unlike mine. It took me years to reach emotional maturity.

I well remember the day in 1947 when my brother came home on leave from the R.A.F. During a few quiet moments together he asked me what I was going to do when I left school. When I said that I did not know he replied, "I've been thinking a lot about this. We've got to get you away from here or you are never going to have any life. You had better apply for a teacher training college." In those few moments the pathway of my future life was decided.

I had no desire to be a school teacher and it still mystifies me how I was ever accepted at a training college. When I asked my headmistress if she would fill in the required forms, she said, "I don't know what to say about you, you are so passive." As a result of the way I was treated in my home that is how I appeared to the outside world. I was incapable of making a decision for myself. In those days schools did not look behind the scenes into the lives of their pupils. I never forgot that word 'passive', but I think my subsequent life has proved her assessment to be rather wide of the mark.

My joy when I received the letter offering me a college place has seldom been equalled. Years later I found an old diary with a ring round 21st September, 1948, which was the date of the first day of my two year course. Every day for six months leading up to that date had been crossed off. I was like a prisoner counting the days till the end of my sentence.

During the forties and fifties training colleges were run more like boarding schools, but to me it was sheer heaven. I became involved in all the activities available, and joined in with great gusto. My years of repression had left me with a zest for life that has stayed with me always.

Suddenly, on 26th November, 1949, I became utterly depressed. My friends were amazed at the change in me but I did not know what was wrong. All was revealed later that day. Theo, my eldest brother arrived to see me. He had to break the news that our beloved brother, Laurie, to whom I was so close, had been killed in a flying accident in far away Malaya. He was twenty-two. I still remember crying out to Theo, "Why is it always us?"

The loss of my brother, who was my champion, was devastating. In the early days I would pretend that it was all a mistake and his tour of duty overseas had been extended.

I could not believe that the unique personality which had been my adored brother could just be extinguished, leaving nothing. The teachings of the orthodox religions gave me no help in coming to terms with this great loss. No one told me it was possible to search for his continued existence on another plane. After reading this book, I trust readers and their families will not have to suffer the desolation and emptiness which I had to undergo. It is possible to find evidence that the parting from your loved one is only temporary.

During my career as a teacher I was drawn to working in a special unit for emotionally disturbed children. My own childhood experiences enabled me to identify with their unhappiness and insecurities. I like to think that my understanding of their pain helped them to grow up into reasonably well adjusted adults. My psychological studies in connection with this work were of great benefit in the handling of patients with anxiety problems during my years as a spiritual healer.

## CHAPTER FIVE

I did not return to live in the family home after I had qualified as a primary school teacher in 1950. The week before my twentieth birthday I took up my first teaching post in a tough area of North London. In the early fifties we were dealing with what was referred to as The Bulge. There was a tremendous rise in the birth-rate in 1945 and 1946 due to the return home of the thousands of men who had been away at the war. It was common to have to deal with classes of forty-five children. Having survived that I could survive anything!

From then on I existed in a variety of 'digs' and bed-sitting rooms. My first month's pay cheque was the princely sum of £20. After paying £10 to my landlady there was precious little left even for necessities such as clothes and bus fares. No one had much money in those days and one didn't have the expectations which young people have in the nineties.

My big dream had always been 'to see the world'. At a party in 1954 I was introduced to a crowd of young Australians who were travelling around Europe. Somehow they sold me the idea of going out to Australia. Within three months I had given in my notice at school, applied and been accepted under the £10 migrant scheme and was setting sail from Tilbury Docks. I didn't have time for second thoughts.

There were a number of young emigrants on board and I soon made new friends. The journey took almost six weeks. When one is cut off from land for days on end the rest of the world ceases to exist. Only the day to day happenings on board ship become important realities.

The new sights, sounds and smells of the places we docked at were very exciting. The unbelievable heat and humidity endured while travelling through the Red Sea in August is still etched on my memory.

When we docked at Colombo, Ceylon (now Sri Lanka), a crowd of us decided to go swimming at a place called Mount Lavinia. It was my first experience of bathing in surf. No sooner had I stepped into the water than I was swept off my feet and felt myself being dragged out to sea. It took every ounce of my strength to battle my way back to the shore, completely exhausted. I had great respect for tropical oceans after that episode.

All good things come to an end and we eventually arrived in Sydney on 16th September, 1954. The dockside was thronged with people there to meet their loved ones, but I knew no one would be waving to me. To this day I can remember the tide of loneliness which swept over me after bidding farewell to all my ship-board friends. I now realize that was one of the lessons I had to learn. Unless you have experienced aloneness on that scale you cannot really appreciate how other lonely people feel. It is one of this worlds problems which I do my best to alleviate whenever possible. With the breaking down of the family unit, there is a whole well of loneliness everywhere now. If you are aware of someone who spends a great deal of time alone, extend the hand of friendship to them. Your own life will be the richer for it.

My destination was Brisbane in Queensland, where I joined the staff of a school. I was in for a shock. It was like returning to a school in England at the turn of the Century. The children were scratching their work on slates and every child in the State was reading the same word on the same page of the same book on the same day. I found this conformity so suffocating that within six months I had given up teaching with no idea what I was going to do to earn my living.

During the next three years I travelled widely throughout the whole country, working my way around. Five months were spent on a cattle station a thousand miles into the Outback. The nearest small settlement consisting of a shop and a hotel was thirty miles from the homestead. The postman came once a week bringing supplies and the week's newspapers. I was part of a way of life which few Australians experience because most of the population live in the cities on the coast.

In Alice Springs I worked in the kitchen of the only hotel. Three times a day I had to wash-up by hand after about a hundred people. My friends called me wrinkled fingers! I believe it is the centre of a thriving tourist industry now.

Hotel work on the islands of the Great Barrier Reef and at Surfer's Paradise on the fabulous Gold Coast of Queensland were unforgettable experiences. One hotel manager even promoted me to the dizzy heights of head waitress.

People often ask me why I left Australia, and I usually reply, "There is more to life than beer and sunshine". The country has changed a great deal over the past forty years, of course, but at that time there was for me a lack of 'depth' to life. I now realize that my experiences there were all part of the lessons which I have had to learn, this time round. This life was not meant to be spent in sunshine.

November, 1957, saw me once again boarding an ocean going liner, but this time my passage had to be paid from money which I had saved while working on the cattle station. I wanted to be able to say that I had been round the world so I chose a ship going via New Zealand and the Panama Canal. We docked at romantic sounding places such as Fiji, Tahiti and Trinidad. Once again one seemed to be in a state of suspended animation. Only the daily trivialities of life on board ship seemed of any consequence.

When one has lived in perpetual sunshine for several years, the actual day to day, practical miseries of an English winter are forgotten. Darkness closing in at four o'clock in the afternoon is very cosy when you have a home and family around you. Huddling over a small gas fire, in yet another bed-sitting room is rather different. Once again I was up against overwhelming loneliness, which led me into a liaison which I deeply regretted. This relationship resulted in the birth of my precious son in May, 1959. I named him Laurence after my beloved brother. At that time it was practically impossible to bring up a child alone without parental support. For me that was out of the question. After much soul-searching and unbelievable heartache, I had to allow him to go for adoption.

Once again the cry, *Why me?*

There are thousands of women of my generation who have had to suffer the same trauma as myself, because of the moral hypocrisy of society in those years before the liberated 'sixties'. When I read now of 360,000 births in one year to single mothers and teenagers being urged on television to have safe sex, I think I must have fallen asleep and woken up on a different planet!

To any woman reading my book who has suffered as I did, I say this. Try to understand that before you came into life this time, you chose to undergo whatever problem you have been obliged to face in the world as it was then. Somewhere there was a learning situation for you, and those around you. See it as one incident in one life amongst an eternity of lives. The heartache and longing never goes away, but a different perspective can help.

If on the other hand you are one of the thousands of children who were adopted, do not be eaten up by feelings of bitterness and resentment against your natural mother. Once again, you knew you were going to be confronted with these problems before you incarnated. It is impossible to measure the reasons for you adoption against a backdrop of society as it is for your generation. Remember, this is only one life.

Several months before my son was born I was living in a home with many other young women in the same situation. Most of them were much younger than myself and they used to come to me seeking advice and to discuss their problems. Sometime afterwards I was telling an elderly friend about this, and she said, "I expect you were meant to be there." At the time I thought it was a very odd remark. It was the first time I had heard anyone suggest that there could be a reason for things which happen to us as we go through life and that there are outside influences over which we have no control. Thirty-five years later it is quite obvious to me that yes, it was all part of the plan of my life which I agreed to before I incarnated.

My insatiable desire to travel was still with me and New Years Day, 1965, saw me stepping off a plane into the 'oven', which is Singapore. Working as a teacher provided the opportunity to visit many countries of the Far East during the school holidays. I was even able to locate my brother's grave in Kuala Lumpur and come to terms with my loss.

Singapore is a multi-cultural society and every type of religion is practised. There is a large Chinese community and although many have converted to Catholicism the old Chinese customs were still observed by many at that time. A firm belief in an after life is very apparent. When a soul passes over, ornate paper houses, cars, boats and especially printed bank notes are burnt for the spirit to take with them into the next world. There are Hindu temples, Buddhist temples, Christian churches and at that time one was woken up early in the morning by the Muslim priest calling to his flock through a loud speaker. There was always a different religious festival taking place but I was unmoved by any of them. At that time any belief beyond the physical was to me a load of poppycock.

Since then the whole world of Spirit has been opened up to me and I now realize how ignorant I was to view all these religious festivals with the patronizing attitude of a tourist. All those devout people of the East are well aware of what it took me nearly fifty years to understand.

However, I like to think my years of travel gave me a breadth of vision encompassing the whole world, which I have been able to draw on in recent years. There is no doubt in my mind that the kaleidoscope of experiences were all part of the plan which I agreed to before incarnating this time. I now realise that if I had had a cosy, comfortable home where I was cherished, my spiritual self would not have reached the level of understanding which it has now attained.

## CHAPTER SIX

"How did you find out that you are spiritual healers," is the question my husband and I are asked more than any other.

It happened in March, 1978, five years after we had married, and just five months after our introduction to Spiritualism. Having visited all the relevant places in the Bristol area we decided it was time to explore our new found interest further afield. We travelled to London to the headquarters of the Spiritualist Association of Great Britain.

During the previous few months, whenever we were at a spiritualist meeting the medium would always pick me out of the congregation for a message from Spirit. It was usually the same theme. They had to tell me that I too was a medium and could do what they were doing. Frankly, I didn't believe them. Mike had never been given any information regarding his spiritual gifts.

We found ourselves in an elite part of London called Belgrave Square. The large porticoed buildings all belong to a by-gone age and there is a genteel atmosphere about the area. The S.A.G.B. (as it is known), is located in one of these elegant buildings, flanked on either side by foreign embassies.

Professional mediums are at work every day, giving private readings. They must demonstrate a very high standard of their gift before being invited to work there. Large rooms are available for public demonstrations of mediumship, lectures and church services. Spiritual healing is regularly available from experienced healers.

On our arrival we were disappointed to learn that all the mediums giving private sittings were fully booked. We were offered a group reading, so we opted for that.

About six of us crowded into a small room with the medium, whose name was Robert Harris-Baird. We shall always remember him because his mediumship completely changed our lives.

We listened intently as he went round the group giving clairvoyant information. One elderly lady, who had obviously been a Spiritualist for many years said to Mr. Harris-Baird, "How much longer do I have to stay here? I've had enough for this time." When she was told there was still spiritual work for her to do she was quite put out and sighed in a very resigned manner.

Her reaction really astounded us, as at that time we were only just beginning to delve into these matters. Our thinking was still very much in the material world and far from the spiritual wavelengths. Here was someone asking when she was going to die and was unhappy at being told that she had to hang on a bit longer. You must agree that this is a refreshing way of looking at life and death. She obviously had no fear of what is generally regarded as the unknown. She was completely satisfied that she knew the truth. She was happy in her knowledge that death is a transition to a different state of consciousness.

When it came to our turn, once more I was told that I was a medium in my own right. He said to me, "Don't be afraid of your own abilities. If you want to prove this, ask your husband to write something on a piece of paper. You will be able to tell him what he has written." When I protested and said, "I've only been interested in this subject for about five months", he replied, "It has probably taken the Spirit World twenty years to create the right conditions for your development."

He then turned to Mike and said, "You know you are a healer?" We were astonished to hear this and my husband had to reply that he didn't know.

"But you must have felt the tingling in your hands", went on Mr. Harris-Baird.

Mike replied, to the amusement of everyone in the room, "Yes, but I put it down to bad circulation."

Although we had realized that healing is an integral part of the Spiritualist philosophy, until then neither of us had taken any interest in it.

We certainly had plenty to talk about on the way home. Later that evening, when we were still discussing the day's events, we decided to try out the suggested test.

Mike thought for a moment and then wrote something on a piece of paper. He could have written anything, couldn't he?

Only one phrase impressed itself on my mind and I said, "Well, all I can think of is, Where are you going"? He showed me the piece of paper, and on it he had written, "Where are you going tomorrow'. I was one word out. We have never tried the test since, in case it was just 'beginners luck'!

To be told that one has the gift of healing is very exciting, but actually developing it is another matter. We had no idea how to set about it. Funnily enough, very soon after our visit to London, I noticed our goldfish Jaws, was down at the bottom of his tank, looking very pale and losing his tail. I said to Mike, "Why don't you try healing the goldfish, I think he is going to die."

Mike placed his hands on either side of the fish tank. The effect was instantaneous. It was as though the fish had been given an electric shock. He shot through the water like a torpedo and never looked back. He lived several years after this episode.

Since we embarked upon our spiritual search there is one aspect of which we are convinced. Nothing happens by accident or chance. So many circumstances have occurred that could not be put down to coincidence. When the spirit world want something to happen, events are made to fall into place.

One night I was glancing through the *Bristol Evening Post* when I saw an advertisement for a course on Spiritual Healing. We do not have this paper on a regular basis, but I happened to buy the issue in which that advertisement was published. Coincidence?

We immediately signed on for the course which was to be held at a healing clinic in another area of Bristol. We had not known of the existence of the clinic until then. After attending lectures for eight weeks we asked if it would be possible for us to join the centre as probationer healers. We were accepted and for the next three years assisted at weekly healing sessions. During this time we obtained our membership of the National Federation of Spiritual Healers.

## CHAPTER SEVEN

I clearly remember the first time I saw the word ' healing'.

I was eleven years old and walking through a country churchyard. On the notice board outside the church, amongst details of the weekly services was written, 'Thursday 11 a.m. HEALING.'

I recall thinking, 'What's that got to do with churches, healing has to do with doctors'.

On another occasion, when I was about twelve, I was out walking with my stepmother and she furtively whispered to me, 'That woman over there is a faith healer'. I remember seeing a perfectly normal woman, but my stepmother made it sound as though she had a disease. I have often wondered, since I became one of these 'odd' people, if the same words have been whispered about myself as I have passed others in the street.

Over the years I had heard or read vague references to spiritual healers but could never have imagined that I would ever join their ranks. Like thousands of others, it would never have occurred to me to seek help from a healer, even if I had known where to find one.

Let me assure everyone who is as ignorant on the subject as I was, that there is nothing mystical about it. There is no reason to feel any apprehension when going to a healer.

Naturally there are differences in the approach of each practitioner but the basic method should be similar.

At the Clinic where we began our healing, Mike and I always worked together as a team and we have continued to do this. A number of married couples operate in this way although healers usually work singly. We have found the arrangement works very well, especially as a male healer should have a chaperone when dealing with female patients.

Healing is another form of mediumhip. Instead of receiving messages from the spirit world the healer is used as a channel to relay healing energies to the patient. These energies are the actual living force within all living things.

The healer is conscious of what I can only describe as a 'presence' in her hands. There is a surge of heat and tingling through the fingertips. The hands are placed on various parts of the body known as 'chakras'. Chakra is an Indian word which denotes an area of the body where the life force may enter and be absorbed.

To begin with she will probably place her hands gently on the top of the patient's head. That area is known as the crown chakra. The healer will close her eyes and tune into her helpers on the spirit side and asked to be used for healing purposes. At the same time it is usual to visualize the patient being whole and healthy again.

After a minute or two the hands will be moved so that one is on the forehead and one at the back of the head. This polarity of the hands is very important. The power meets in the centre of the patient. This applies also when two healers are working on the same patient. One works at the front and the other from the back. The next position will probably be one hand on the chest and the other in the centre of the back. Moving down, the next area will be one hand on the solar plexus and the other at the bottom of the spine. When the healer has covered the whole body in this manner, including each end of the spinal column, she will then concentrate the power on the seat of the problem.

The patient is only required to close her eyes and relax to the best of her ability, erecting no mental barriers. The popular phrase 'faith healing' is wrong – faith has nothing to do with this. We are talking about spiritual power sent from Spirit, through the spirit of the healer to the spirit of the patient. The recipient may feel heat, she may feel vibration or she may feel nothing.

Some patients tell us that it is like having hot water bottles placed all over them, while others drift away so deeply that it takes a minute or two for them to return to us. Occasionally a patient has been completely unaware that we have been playing gentle background music, so deep has been their relaxation. The build up of spiritual power in the room is so great that particularly sensitive patients have become clairvoyant during their healing session and have been aware of loved ones and Guides.

I will now try to clarify what has been taking place.

We each have two identical bodies, the physical and the etheric. The latter is the one which returns to the spirit world when we die, leaving the physical behind. Illness occurs when the two bodies are not in harmony. The purpose of healing is to rectify this and help the physical body to heal itself. Stress and tension are two of the underlying causes of illness in the modern world and we often have people come to us and say, "I want my battery recharged."

To the sceptic the idea of someone tuning into an invisible spiritual force is laughable. I know. Don't forget, I belonged to the 'load of rubbish' brigade for over forty years.

Let us look at it logically. No-one is surprised these days that radio and television sets pick up unseen signals. A hundred years ago it would have been looked upon as sheer magic.

Do you see anything when you put your frozen pizza in the microwave oven? It comes our cooked doesn't it?

You do not doubt the presence of electricity even though the power is not visible. The only sign that it exists is the resulting hot water when you plug in your kettle.

Wind cannot be seen, only the devastation left behind when it gets out of control.

There are special whistles for dogs which make sounds beyond the range of human hearing. The sound must be there because the dogs react to it.

There are many other phenomena which cannot be experienced via the five human senses, but can be proved to exist through scientific means. So why should it not be possible for there to be other energies which certain human beings are able to tune into, in order to bring relief from suffering.

On a deeper level, we are told by the spirit philosopher Silver Birch that the object of healing is not necessarily to mend the physical body, but to touch the soul. When healing has been experienced to some degree, the receiver begins to ask questions and wonder about the source of the energy which achieved this noticeable change in their whole condition. The course of their lives may be changed. Some healers are working today as a result of experiencing their own return to health by way of spiritual power.

One of the criteria for being a successful healer is the ability to feel compassion for others. We learn compassion from having suffered ourselves in this life and previous lives. You will seldom find a healer who has had an easy passage.

Healers must never be judgmental, whatever the circumstances which bring patients to them. It is important that those handing over the healing power never lose sight of the fact that they are only instruments for the transference of divine energy, and not the source of it. Mike and I see ourselves as postmen, handing over what is sent.

## CHAPTER EIGHT

During 1982 we decided it was time for us to branch out on our own. We had our own ideas on how a place of healing should be run. At the Centre where we did our probation, the healing had been conducted on a dais in front of all the other waiting patients. Since illness is a private matter, we felt that whatever is said and done should not be carried out in public. Relaxation is a vital factor in the healing process and no one can feel at ease in front of a crowd of people. In some Spiritualist Churches patients are treated after the evening service while other members of the church are clattering around with cups and saucers. It takes concentration in the correct atmosphere to achieve the best results.

The smallest bedroom in our bungalow was turned into a Healing Sanctuary. Twelve years later it is still only used for our spiritual work. The atmosphere in the room is entirely different from when it was used as a bedroom. This is due to the build up of spiritual power over the years.

Colours vibrate and blue is the vibration of healing. Therefore, we decorated the room with suitably patterned, restful wallpaper. A blue carpet was put down and blue velvet curtains, donated by a grateful patient, were hung at the windows. A dimmer switch, to provide a more restful atmosphere, was installed by another delighted patient. Special stools, chairs and a table on which there is always an arrangement of flowers were purchased.

One day while discussing the room with a particularly spiritual friend, I mentioned that I wanted to buy a picture for the wall, but had no idea what to look for. She said, "How about a bluebell wood?" That sounded a marvellous suggestion, but the possibility of finding anything like it, seemed very remote.

On the Saturday morning that we decided to go out and look for the picture, the postman brought me a cheque for £50 from the Premium Bonds. That seemed like a good start to the day.

The gentleman who had taken our wedding photographs ten years earlier had a picture gallery and we decided to begin our search there. While my husband chatted to him I walked to the back room where the pictures were displayed.

Wandering through the doorway, I received an electrifying shock as my eyes lighted on a large painting displayed on an easel in front of me. It was entitled 'Bluebell Walk'. The scene depicted a pathway through a bluebell wood, alongside a gently flowing stream. The subject matter could not have been more appropriate if we had especially commissioned it. Needless to say we bought the picture and it still has pride of place in the Sanctuary.

Could our visit to that particular shop have been just coincidence?

For several months we had been giving treatment to friends in our home, so when we opened the Sanctuary they continued to come, together with a number who had become our special patients at the Clinic. From this small beginning our work for Spirit blossomed. Word got around that we held healing sessions on a certain evening and anyone could come along and let themselves in. One evening we came out of the Sanctuary, having dealt with the first patient, to find about ten people squeezed into our lounge. Since each session takes at least fifteen minutes, with the two of us working together, it meant that the last person to arrive had over two hours to wait. It was then we realized there would have to be an appointments diary. The healing sessions then extended to two nights a week and we were sometimes seeing as many as sixteen patients on each evening. Gradually as health problems diminished the numbers became more manageable, but there has always been a steady stream of people coming to us by word of mouth recommendation. We have never advertised because we feel that if Spirit want us to treat someone then a way will be found for them to hear about our work.

When a person seeks out a healer they are usually at the end of their tether, having been told by the medical profession that they have got to 'live with their condition'. They are willing to try anything to get relief from their suffering.

So, when a new patient comes along to us we first of all introduce ourselves and give some background information regarding our professional jobs. We try to show that apart from our gift we are reasonably normal human being, and don't have horns on our heads!

The next thing we say is, "We can't promise you anything. We only hand over what is sent for you."

Having made that clear we usually go on to point out that we will be surprised and disappointed if there is no improvement in their condition. I can't recall anyone who has felt that they have received no benefit, even if it is only a lessening of the extreme tension, brought on by their problem.

Many tears of relief have been shed in our Sanctuary by both men and women. Numerous secret heartaches and worries have been voiced which could never have been mentioned in a public place. Fears and problems which would have stayed locked up inside the sufferers, causing further distress, unhappiness and illness.

People who do not understand what we are endeavouring to do, confuse the words healing and curing. Doctors attempt to cure specific ailments by means of drugs and surgery. They cannot promise a full recovery either, because their work is sometimes a case of trial and error.

A healer deals with the whole person, body, mind and spirit. We aim to complement the work of the medical profession, not take its place. The suggestion would never be made that a patient should stop seeing her doctor or cease taking prescribed drugs. The relief of human suffering should be a combined operation.

First and foremost, as I mentioned earlier, but it bears emphasising again, the healer is only the instrument, and not the provider of the healing energies. We know there is a band of helpers on the spirit side who channel specific rays through us to treat specific problems. We have been told that many of our assistants were doctors when they were on this side of life. An experienced healer is aware of different types and strengths of energy being channelled. Sometimes there is a tremendous concentration of power on one eye, or across the shoulders where there is a build up of tension. If there is difficulty in walking the force of the power may be concentrated on the spine, because that is the seat of the problem, not the legs.

Over the years Mike has developed a strong diagnostic link with our spirit band. He instinctively knows where to place his hands even though the patient may have made no mention of having problems in a certain area.

Many people who come to us have been ill for a long time. Consequently they are depressed and at a very low ebb. In our experience the mental state is dealt with first. The spirits (no pun intended) of the patient are lifted so that she is better able to cope with her problem. As we always say, it is no good getting rid of someone's bad back if they are so depressed that they jump off the nearest bridge.

Some patients arrive as taut as piano wires, declaring that it is impossible for them to relax. These are often the ones who, by the end of their treatment, are weeping with profound relief. They have been able to let go of tension which, in some cases, they have been carrying around for years.

Our first healing success came very soon after we began working at the Clinic. A professional lady, who had suffered from regular bouts of migraine over many years, began to realize after a few weeks that the ferocity of the attacks was diminishing. She no longer had to take days off work at regular intervals, as she had been forced to do in the past. We were as thrilled as she was at this success, and as far as I know the severe attacks did not return.

In 1982 one young woman was so delighted with her healing that she wrote to *Psychic News* about it and her story was published. As far back as 1974 she had been diagnosed as suffering from osteoarthritis/cervical spondylitis. She was in constant pain and could only get through the day by taking many painkillers.

After she had healing from our band of helpers she wrote as follows:-

"For the first time in years in addition to my full time job I did all my housework, shopping, washing and gardening. I cleaned both my car and my husband's in one afternoon. In 1981 we had a fortnight's holiday when, for the first time in years I didn't care what the bed was like. We walked for miles and it was the best holiday of our lives."

In 1984 this lady gave birth to a healthy baby girl. Carrying a child for nine months would have been out of the question before she was healed.

I remember one middle aged lady who was delighted when she could get out of the bath properly, after her arthritis showed so much improvement.

A gentleman who had had tinnitus (noises in the ears and head) for forty years, was completely cured. He said he kept wondering what was missing.

Another gentleman suffered from psoriasis for twenty five years after being involved in a grenade attack while serving with the forces overseas. He was so amazed when his symptoms began to vanish that he said he must go and ask his doctor about it. We found this faintly amusing since the medical profession had been trying to cure him for a quarter of a century.

When one becomes a healer there are many other aspects which must be taken into consideration. It is not just a case of putting ones hands on another person's head. Several times a week we sit together, tune into our band of helpers and read out the names on what is called our absent healing list. This may include people far away, whom we have never met, but whose names have been given to us by concerned relatives and friends.

The telephone is likely to ring at all kinds of odd times. For instance, one Boxing Day we were called out twice to two different desperate souls. No one forces us to go, of course, but having committed ourselves to the work it does not occur to us to refuse.

Those suffering from severe depression are frequent callers in between healing sessions. Sometimes I have felt like a one-woman Samaritan organization. There have been times when I have been afraid to bring the conversation to a close in case the caller committed suicide. In these cases we lend a listening ear and let them know that someone cares. Fortunately these situations only occur very occasionally. However, becoming a healer is not something that can be taken lightly. The more experience one has of the real world the better one is able to support others at times of crisis in their lives.

Naturally a number of terminally ill patients have sought our help. We are all going to die one day, and if it is time for a soul to return to the spirit world, no amount of healing is going to stop this from happening. However, in our experience, those souls who are nearing the end of this earthly life find great peace and comfort from healing and they have a gentle transition into the next phase of their existence. That is what we mean by the phrase, treating the whole person, body, mind and spirit. We are able to dispel any fears which they might have regarding the manner of their passing.

At this point, while discussing terminal illness it is appropriate to mention that my husband nursed his first wife for three years through cancer. At that time he knew nothing about spiritual healing, and when she died he certainly received no solace from the orthodox church. We know now, that his experiences then were part of his apprenticeship for the work which we had been chosen to do together, twenty years on.

Silver Birch tells us that often a healer's greatest successes are with those who pass on. We like to think that is true in so far as our late patients are concerned.

Since I began writing these memoirs I have been in touch with some of our past patients. I asked them to write a few lines about their own healing and the effect that it had on their lives since then. I felt it would be more meaningful to quote from the patients themselves, rather than give my own description of what took place.

I shall devote the next chapter to extracts from these letters.

## CHAPTER NINE

The first ex-patient I tracked down was the mother of four children, and I shall refer to her as Penny.

Penny came to us over a period of ten months in 1983, and we have always regarded her healing as one of our most rewarding.

I discovered she was now living near Oxford and during the intervening ten years she had given birth to a daughter, Alex, in 1991. Penny was pleased to be of assistance and wrote at great length for me. The following is an extract of what she had to say.

"I had been feeling off colour for some time. My left arm and side would develop pins and needles, go numb and ache. One day a friend at work asked why my hand was almost pale green. It looked dead and had no feeling in it. I could ignore the symptoms no longer and went to my doctor.

I underwent a series of tests at the hospital, and was eventually told that I had M.S. (multiple sclerosis). At that stage I did not really know what M.S. was. I was treated with steroids but things did not improve. I felt the cold terribly at work and was forced to tell my boss the reason for this. He promised not to inform our superiors and provided me with an electric fire.

Shortly after this, my boss approached me and asked in an embarrassed way if I thought healing worked. He went on to say that he knew someone who might be able to help.

Although not sure if I believed healing could do anything, I felt it was worth a try. Nothing else had helped so I had nothing to lose.

I was surprised to discover that the healer worked in the same building as myself, but he seemed a normal, caring person. I'm not sure what I imagined him to be like – I had never thought about healers before. I arranged to go to his home, where he and his wife gave treatment.

The first time I went I was made to feel comfortable and relaxed. I heard Mike's voice telling me to put aside my problems for a few minutes and visualize my favourite flower. I drifted away. I felt peaceful as though floating, but still attached to the ground. I awoke feeling relaxed and contented. That night I had the best nights sleep I had had in years.

This was the first of many healing sessions, and after each one I felt happy and free from pain.

During the sessions I became aware of people who seemed real and I could hold conversations with them in my head. I saw my Grandfather who had loved and protected me as a child. He said he had been waiting for me to come. He wanted me to learn and benefit from his experiences. He said I must come as often as possible and I would be cured. Gradually he introduced others who wished to speak to me.

There was a nurse in a grey uniform named Frances, followed by a bearded gentleman, named Samuel. Samuel is special. He led me into a beautiful garden where the serenity offered total peace of body and mind. He still allows me to use him for advice, answers questions, but never dictates. He maintains the role of Guide – not a fixer of things the way I want them. Although I am an adult I feel as though I am still at school. Samuel is a teacher who opens the gate but allows me to choose which path to follow.

From the first time I received healing my health improved. Over a period of time I became aware that the pain did not recur between sessions. One memorable day I touched the kettle and felt the resulting pain. I did it again to prove to myself that the feeling was coming back into my hands. My doctor said she did not understand what I was doing, but what ever it was, not to stop! I was able to lengthen the time between sessions until I realized I no longer needed healing – I was whole again.

I still communicate with my friends 'on the other side'. I have learnt that there is a purpose to all things which happen to us in life. Most of them are pre-determined before conception. We are all travelling along a road which is uphill and we each need different experiences to enable us to progress. I believe our souls never die but live on and continue development.

Sensitive people are able to look into the eyes of a small child and know that she is 'an old soul'. By that I mean someone who has been back many times and has travelled a long way along life's road. That comment was made about my youngest daughter by a nurse in the children's cardiac ward of our local hospital.

Alex was born with many problems, (I refuse to call them handicaps because her personality was so strong). They were not a handicap to her enjoyment of her short life.

When she was born part of the brain lining protruded through her skull and it had to be sealed immediately. We also discovered that she had no ovaries, so her development as a female would need hormone treatment. At ten days she had a second operation to drain excess fluid from her brain. She appeared to thrive, but at eleven weeks she was rushed to hospital and she was found to have five chambers to her heart and all the arteries and veins were in the wrong place.

Major heart surgery was carried out, and she survived against all the odds. Four days later she had a hernia operation.

We felt that all the forces in the universe were helping us. People told us she was born for a reason. Her strength shone through and captured the hearts of doctors, nurses, relatives and friends. Everyone felt she was special.

Just when it seemed she had beaten all her problems she had a cardiac arrest and was rushed to intensive care. Major surgery was carried out immediately. She survived this operation, but had two further cardiac arrests over the next few days. Doctors and nurses fought to save her.

She was conscious and her eyes held a wisdom greater than mine. There was nothing any of us could do except pray. I knew I was going to lose my little girl but I understood that her task was complete.

She died in my arms when the moment was right for her.

I felt my husband's mother, who had died before we were married, standing next to me. I heard her say, "I'll take care of her, she's coming home now."

I firmly believe that Alex had a job to do here and she fulfilled her mission. She is now free from pain and has gone to continue her spiritual progress.

Alex enriched us all despite only being here for six months. She influenced many people and had a dramatic effect on many lives. So much concern for others was stimulated by her plight, which would never have happened if she had been born whole.

Doctors, surgeons and nurses learned a great deal from working with Alex, and others who come after will have richer lives as a result of their experiences with her."

In her covering letter to me Penny said that although she felt all the grief of a parent she felt privileged to have been chosen by an 'old soul' such as Alex, She knows it was necessary to have been made aware of Samuel through her own healing, so that he could help her with her acceptance of the situation. Given the choice she would go through it all again because she is convinced that everything we suffer in life has a purpose.

I read the story of Alex with tears in my eyes, while at the same time feeling humble and delighted that Mike and I had been chosen to play a role in those events.

## SUSAN

The next person I contacted was pleased to contribute her story and I shall refer to her as Susan. I do not include her words for self-aggrandisement but as an example of what can be achieved through spiritual healing. She wrote as follows:-

"What makes two people give hours of their time for no monetary reward, to a continual flow of strangers through their front door?

The answer is that these two ordinary people have the extraordinary gift of healing.

I first met Beth and Mike five years ago when I turned to them for help after being diagnosed as having cancer. The slight feeling of uncertainty I experienced that first evening quickly disappeared as they put me at my ease, and explained about healing over a cup of tea.

In their Sanctuary, where the healing takes place, I felt warmth, energy and peace flowing into my body.

My Consultant was amazed at my progress. Although I was having chemotherapy I firmly believe that I would not have coped as well or returned to health so quickly had it not been for the healing I received.

I attended healing sessions every week for five years. During this time I gained a new spiritual outlook on life and became a more confident and whole person.

As healers, Mike and Beth always stress that they only act as channels for the healing forces, but they also give unfailingly of their time, care and love.

This was demonstrated when my only daughter was seriously ill with meningitis. The doctors said they could do no more and my daughter was slipping away in a coma.

I rang Mike and Beth and they made two visits to the hospital that evening, giving healing to Jenny and comfort to me. Within a short while the miracle of my daughter's recovery began. She is now fully fit with none of the side effects which can so tragically affect the sufferers of this disease.

To sum up: I truly believe that the healing energy which flowed from my healers into myself and my daughter played a very large part in our recovery. I shall always be indebted and grateful to these two kind people whom I regard as my friends for life."

## PAM

The next contributor was a lady I shall refer to as Pam.

Pam was caring for her two year old grandson in 1982, when she contacted us. She writes as follows:-

"One Saturday evening as I undressed my grandson, Paul, I noticed a very large black bruise on his ankle. I asked his mother how it got there, but she said she had no idea. As his clothes came off I noticed more and more bruises on his body. While he was in his bath bruises were appearing as we watched.

I rang my doctor who came immediately. After examining Paul, the G.P. said it may not be what he thought it was, but to be prepared. He thought it was leukaemia, but I was not to tell my daughter until it was confirmed.

I telephoned Mike and Beth and they said I could bring Paul over straight away. Normally Paul would never go near strangers but he took their hands and walked into the Sanctuary with them, without looking back. Later Mike and Beth told us that he sat on the stool to be treated without moving – a feat I would have said was totally impossible for Paul.

We remembered that he had been rather listless and pale for a few days and not his usual lively self. On Monday morning we took him to Frenchay Hospital for tests. During the next three days he had two more healing sessions and all the bruises were fading. He began to return to his old mischievous self.

When we plucked up courage to ring the doctor for the test results we were told that he wanted to see us straightaway. A bad omen we thought.

As we walked into the surgery we could see the doctor smiling. "No Leukaemia present", he said. I asked him if he had definitely thought it was leukaemia and he said he had been certain. The tests indicated that Paul's blood had undergone a massive change, with dead corpuscles everywhere.

Later, when Paul was completely free I told my G.P. about the healing. His reaction was that he believed it, because he had seen such recoveries before."

Mike and I were especially thrilled at the outcome of this healing since Pam was the person who had kept on insisting that we make our first visit to a Spiritualist Church.

Life as a healer is full of surprises.

During 1991, a large parcel was delivered to us. The stamps indicated that it was posted in the U.S.A., but we were sure we did not know anyone in America. Inside there were three lovely bath towels, with a covering letter which said, "Good day, I hope I find you. I expect you must be saying that you don't remember me. I came to you for healing when I was on holiday in England staying with my cousin Mrs. Brown. On my return to New York I was to have had an operation on my eyes. Thanks be to God I am much better now and do not need the operation."

# EDNA

In a previous chapter I mentioned absent healing, and the following is an account which we received from Edna, in Yorkshire.

"From November, 1990 to March, 1991, I had suffered the after effects of a common cold. This included deafness in my left ear, and my G.P. was treating me for an infection.

On 12th March, a swelling appeared on the lymph gland on the left side of my neck. Arrangements were made for me to see the E.N.T. specialist, and the appointment took place on 19th April. In the interim the swelling had become larger.

I was given a thorough examination and many tests were made. The result was that on 22nd April, I was admitted to hospital where an exploratory examination revealed a 'growth' on the back of my tongue and also a large yellow 'ball'. They were having difficulty seeing if the two were joined together. Speaking to me, the specialist said he would like me to have a 'scan' before operating, "I haven't got the big C have I?" I asked. "I'm afraid so", was the reply. I was devastated. You never dream these things will happen to you.

I had to wait until 9th May for my turn on the 'scanner' and another fortnight for the results. During those weeks I became a nervous wreck despite medication from my doctor. I was going to die! Would I see another Christmas! The thoughts which raced through my mind were overwhelming. I could still feel this large swelling in my neck.

Out of the blue, a phone call from my niece Pat, who lives far away in Gloucestershire. She told me about Beth and Mike, two people unknown to me, who were praying for me. It was unbelievable to think that strangers were coming to my rescue.

From the moment I put the phone down, I saw the swelling gradually disappear, and over the course of the next few days disappear altogether.

On 23rd May, the Specialist showed me the Scan results which clearly indicated two large lumps. He could not understand how the swelling had disappeared so quickly. His colleagues were dumbfounded.

To satisfy himself he did another exploratory operation taking the 'growth' from the back of my tongue along with snippets from all the glands in my throat. He sent them for a biopsy, and the results all proved negative. He admitted he was baffled.

He could see no reason not to discharge me. His concluding words were that he was absolutely mystified. Should I have told him, I wonder?"

## CHAPTER TEN

Before leaving the subject of healing I want to introduce a beautiful, curly haired blonde, named Truus. This particular blonde was a large, shaggy, adorable member of the canine family.

I first made Truus' acquaintance several years ago whilst walking my own dogs. She was always accompanied by her mother, a black mongrel called Nippy and her owner, Toni. Truus' owner comes from Holland and Truus is a common Dutch Christian name.

Truus and I struck up an instant rapport. Whenever we met in our dog-walking field she would always shamble over to pass the time of day with me.

One day, during 1988, I met Toni in the field and Truus was some distance away, walking very slowly. Toni said, "Truus wants to tell you Auntie that she was attacked by two alsatians. She is still in such a state of shock that she can hardly walk. I even had to lift her over the stile into the field."

*The lovely 'Truus' enjoying the garden as her health improved.*

I walked down the field to Truus and stroked her. She then proceeded to lie down in front of me and I put my hands on her. Healing energy began to flow. After a few minutes I took my hands away but she put up her paw to ask me to continue. A few minutes passed and then she stood up, shook herself, trotted down the field, jumped over the stile and went home.

Meanwhile Toni just stared in amazement. I explained that I was a healer, but she found it difficult to believe what she had just seen with her own eyes.

Truus was perfectly well after that and whenever we met in the field she never failed to come over to be stroked and patted.

Time went on and Nippy grew so old and ill that she had to be put to sleep. Truus, being an extremely sensitive creature was devastated by the death of her mother and grieved to the depths of her being. Within a few weeks the vet diagnosed cancer of the liver. She was given only a few weeks to live. The only treatment the vet could offer were vitamin injections.

When this happened Toni immediately remembered the healing in the field a few years previously. As we only met in the field she did not know where I lived and had no way of contacting me. Eventually one very wet and windy day our dog-walking coincided and she was able to tell me of Truus' plight. I promised to visit her at home the next day.

She was a very sick dog and lay on her blanket shivering continuously. Her tummy was swollen and red from the cancer and she had bad diarrhoea.

Truus knew why I was there and was as good as gold while I treated her. It was obvious that she was extremely ill. I had to say to Toni and her husband, that while we must always be optimistic, it might be that at twelve years of age the healing was meant to ease her passing into Spirit.

I enlisted Mike's help and for several months we visited her twice weekly. Gradually the shivering stopped and the diarrhoea cleared up. Her front elbows which had rubbed red raw from lying about, healed up. Although her tummy was still swollen, the redness disappeared. The yellow in her eyes, indicating a liver condition was no longer visible.

The vet was clearly puzzled and kept referring to his notes of blood counts and could not understand how he could have made such a wrong diagnosis.

Best of all her behaviour returned to what it had been before Nippy's death. We were all thrilled when she barked at a passing stranger. She began doing all the little things which were peculiar to her. She began carrying slippers and balls about and insisted on going to the pub with her Master in the evening. Each week showed a further improvement in her condition and the quality of her life.

Six months after she should have died she spent Christmas in a hotel.

Truus died of old age almost a year after the vet's diagnosis gave her no chance of survival. She was an old lady in doggie terms, and I am convinced this healing had a deep purpose behind it. Her owners have connections in Holland, Canada, Australia and several other countries. Many, many people who would never have heard about spiritual healing are aware of Truus' miraculous recovery and are asking questions.

Even the vet referred to her as 'The Miracle Dog'.

I am reminded of two other dogs who have caused their vets to raise their eyebrows in surprise.

Phoebe was a lovely old long-bodied Basset who had terrible back trouble. She was in such a bad way that her owners carried her about on a folded up deck chair as a stretcher. The vet said nothing could be done for her.

We visited her at her home. As we worked on her we could both feel the bones of her spine moving beneath our fingers. Her condition improved immediately. When she walked back into the surgery the vet refused to believe it was the same dog.

Sashi, a Lhasa Apso had always been a problem dog, He was a poor eater and had constant tummy problems. The vet could find nothing physically wrong with him.

One evening while we were being entertained in his home, he jumped up onto my husband's lap. Mike immediately felt the need for healing and placed his hands on Sashi's tummy. He lay there for a considerable time, obviously enjoying the sensation of the healing power being put through him. His eating problem vanished and after visiting us at home twice more he was a different dog.

My own cat Sally was another little miracle. I noticed an angry looking growth on one of her paws and took her to the vet. He said it was quite common in cats and it would have to be removed under anaesthetic. I made an appointment for about a week ahead when I knew I would not be at work.

The next day she was snoozing on my lap and I decided I might as well try to give her some healing on the bad paw. I held it for a while and then I must admit, thought nothing more about it.

On the day of the appointment I tried to inspect the paw but she wouldn't let me. I popped her into the basket and took her off to the surgery.

After I had been home for about half an hour the phone rang. I recognised the voice on the other end and my heart sank. I was sure my beloved Sally must have died under the anaesthetic. I couldn't believe it when the voice said, "Which paw is the growth supposed to be on? We can't find any sign of a growth anywhere!"

I hope these examples answer clearly the question which we are always being asked, "Do you have to have faith in order to be healed?"

Animals are not affiliated to any man-made organization. They instinctively know that healing energies come from a Divine Source and erect no barriers. As humans we can learn a great deal from our brothers and sisters in the animal kingdom.

## CHAPTER ELEVEN

Mediumship is looked upon as something mysterious or even sinister by many people. I hope to be able to dispel these archaic attitudes and bring the understanding of this age-old talent into the twentieth, or perhaps I should now say, the twenty-first century.

The popular image of a medium is either a gypsy staring into a crystal ball or an old lady in a darkened room, holding hands with a group of others, saying, "Is anybody there?"

Both impressions are quite wrong. To begin with many Spiritualist mediums are young and many are also male. They are not fortune tellers working on the psychic level. They are men and women who have developed their psychic sensitivity to such a degree that they are able to tune into the higher vibrations of the etheric world. Their job is to provide a channel for those in spirit who wish to communicate with their loved ones still on earth: to prove that life goes on in another dimension. The phrase which one hears in association with mediumship, 'calling up the dead' could not be more wrong. To start with those on the 'other side of life' are still very much alive and the communication is set up from their side, not ours. The medium just makes herself available to be used – she cannot 'call up' anybody.

By visiting a Spiritualist medium for a private sitting or going to a Spiritualist church, a person is providing the conditions necessary for their loved ones to communicate with them, if they so wish. I have had people say to me, 'My Mum's never got in touch with me', or words to that effect, when they admit that they have never been anywhere to create the link.

The underlying reason for receiving a message from a loved one is to prove that the departed soul has not vanished for ever, and still cares what happens to you. Messages are as varied as the number of people giving and receiving them. You may have evidence regarding a problem which you are facing at that time, about which the medium could not possibly have any knowledge. You may be given a memory of something which took place during your childhood, which perhaps only your mother knew about. The medium may describe the person who is communicating and give details of their personality. The accuracy of your message depends on how well developed the medium is and how good your loved one is at communicating.

When visiting a Spiritualist Church, or attending a public meeting held perhaps in a theatre you will usually witness what comes under the general heading of mental mediumship. Most people are familiar with the words clairvoyance and clairaudience, which mean clear seeing and clear hearing. The sensitive, which is another word for medium, sees pictures in her mind, which have been relayed by her Guides, or hears voices from the spirit vibrations. That, of course, is over simplifying a complex procedure. The majority of mediums are skilled in both forms of communication. The late Doris Stokes was an accomplished clairaudient but she could also 'see'.

There is another ingredient possessed by these talented people, which is sometimes referred to as clairsentience. This means the ability to 'feel' conditions through their sensitivity, rather than being told them. It is a sixth sense, rather like intuition. There is a skill known as psychometry, when the sensitive handles a personal possession, for instance, and is able to pick up information about the object and its owner.

Most of the extremely gifted people in the mediumistic field have been aware of spirit influences in their lives since childhood. A dramatic event or a tragedy often triggers off their willingness to accept and use the talent with which they were born.

In order to develop one's mediumistic gift it is necessary to sit in what is known as a development circle under the guidance of a fully fledged medium. During this time the would-be sensitive becomes aware of her Guide, who has chosen to work with her during her mediumship years. The Guide's job, during a demonstration, is to sort out those 'on the other side' who are clamouring to communicate and to let the medium know who the recipient of the message is going to be. After all, if a medium is working in a large theatre holding about eight hundred people its no good her standing up and saying, "Does anybody know Bill?"

Perhaps someone reading this book may have 'odd' experiences and not understand what is happening to them. You may look at a stranger and 'know' something about the person without being given the information verbally. Do not be afraid. Who knows, you might be meant to become the outstanding medium of the 21st Century. Anyone who feels strongly that they have a latent talent for this work should enquire at their local Spiritualist Church, where there will be a weekly development circle.

Mediumship manifests in many different forms. Some talented people, known as psychic artists are able to draw a portrait of the soul who is communicating. Often at a public meeting a clairvoyant will share the platform and tune in to the same entity. She will give the verbal message which goes with the drawing. Coral Polge is one of our most gifted psychic artists at this time and her book, *The Living Image* is highly recommended.

On a similar theme, a lady named Rosemary Brown writes music which is channelled through her by famous composers. Experts have verified that the compositions are in the exact style of the musician named, for example Liszt. Her book, *Look Beyond Today* is another interesting read.

There are two types of writing under spirit guidance.

One is known as Automatic Writing, in which the medium holds the pen and the writing is done by spiritual power.

The other is called Inspirational Writing, in which the writer is impressed with thoughts by her Guides. The following is an example of inspirational writing received by myself on 24th April, 1991, during the time I have been writing these memoirs.

"Do not imagine that you can discover the secrets of 'life' over-night. It takes much searching, but in the searching you learn and grow spiritually. Each step is a grain of sand towards the sea of understanding that awaits you. As the waves lap on the sea shore, gradually a little more of the sand is uncovered as the tide of ignorance recedes. Go forward with the tide."

I am satisfied that those words did not come from myself.

There is another class of communication known as Physical Mediumship. Under this heading there are many different ways in which those in the spirit world communicate.

Each night of the week, up and down the country, interested people gather together to make contact with the etheric world.

Many people will have heard of 'Trance' and find the idea of it frightening. When you understand what is happening and have witnessed the phenomenon you realise there is nothing fearful about it.

Trance manifests on many levels. Sometimes the Guide just overshadows the medium enough to impress her with philosophical or factual thoughts to pass on to those listening. At the other end of the scale the medium goes deeply asleep. Her spirit moves out to allow the Guide to temporarily take over the physical body. Very often the voice, features and bearing of the medium change to that of the communicating Guide. Afterwards, when the entity has finished speaking and the medium is back to normal, she does not know what has taken place while she has been asleep.

One of our most famous trance mediums was Maurice Barbanell, who passed to spirit in 1987.

In 1932 as a young Fleet Street reporter, he set out to expose and ridicule Spiritualism. Far from exposing it, he was so convinced by what he discovered that he founded a weekly newspaper, called *Psychic News*. He continued to be its editor until his death.

For over forty years, 'Barbie', as he was affectionately known, was the trance medium at the home circle of Hannen Swaffer, another famous Fleet street editor of the 30's and 40's.

His Guide, a North American Indian named Silver Birch, is one of Spiritualism's most famous philosophers. His words of wisdom have been published in many books and his eloquent prose translated into several languages. Anyone wishing to begin the study of the Spiritualist philosophy of Truth, need look no further than the books of Silver Birch, published by *Psychic Press*. Tape recordings made at the seances are also available. They are compulsive listening.

There is a spirit manufactured substance known as ectoplasm, which issues rather like a thick vapour, from a deeply entranced medium. This material is used by those working on the spirit side to create more incredible forms of communication.

Ectoplasm is used for what is known as 'direct voice' communication. The workers in spirit fashion a voice box to one side of the entranced medium. The communicators from spirit are able to speak to their loved ones, using their own recognisable voices, via this instrument.

The most well-known exponent of this type of mediumship is Leslie Flint, who unfortunately has now retired. I have not had the good fortune to witness his direct voice phenomena, but I have heard tape recordings made during his seances.

The actress Ellen Terry was one famous person who communicated when the recording was made and her beautiful rounded tones were in complete contrast to the broad Scots accent of John Brown, about whom there was so much scandal at the court of Queen Victoria. In actual fact John Brown was a remarkable medium who kept the then Queen in touch with her beloved Albert. He spoke scathingly about the aristocracy at Court who looked down on him for his uncouth behaviour. He admitted that he often drank too much Scotch whisky on purpose, in order to offend them.

Leslie Flint's book, *Voices in the Dark*, is a fascinating read.

Ectoplasm is also used by the spirit workers to change the features of an entranced medium into those of the communicating spirit. This is known as transfiguration.

However, the most remarkable form of physical mediumship is known as materialization. At these seances the spirit bodies of the communicating souls are clothed in ectoplasm so that they may be recognised by those present. Since this form of mediumship is so important because it provides solid proof of survival of physical death, I shall devote a separate chapter to it.

## CHAPTER TWELVE

It is probably difficult for most people who have never investigated the spiritual side of life to believe that there is any connection between the 'goings on' in a seance room and the work of a scientist in his laboratory. We all tend to put the knowledge we accumulate as we go through life into separate compartments in our minds. If we look deeply enough many subjects are linked and overlap each other. I will try to explain in simple language how these two seemingly different topics fit into the same pigeonhole.

For over a hundred years scientists have been investigating the remarkable psychic phenomenon known as materialization. This is the source from which the ultimate proof of 'life after death' will come. From scientific investigation carried out by eminent physicists, we shall obtain undeniable evidence that we all survive physical death, regardless of whether or not we have carried out the rituals of the various man-made religions.

In my mind these experiments should be divided into two sections. The years of investigation before the splitting of the atom constitute the first part, followed by the half century since that remarkable achievement. I have never studied physics at any level, therefore my explanations will only be rudimentary. The aim of this book is to open eyes and minds while providing a window to the wonders which exist in our universe.

To begin with it must be understood that everything in our world is made up of atoms. We cannot see them because to our eyes all we survey appears to be solid. For centuries scientists believed that the atom was the smallest piece of matter in creation. During the 1930's and 40's physicists worked hard to break down the atom into even more minute particles. In so doing they discovered hitherto unimaginable energies, which resulted in the construction of the first atom bomb. We are all aware of the awesome destructive power of that single piece of equipment. At that level of experimentation physics is closely linked with advanced mathematics, and these discoveries were made through mathematical formulae, i.e. those 'sums' which professors do which look like Chinese to the majority of mortals. As a schoolgirl I recall my brothers trying to enlighten me regarding the mysteries of scientific formulae, but a glazed expression would come into my eyes and they abandoned their efforts to educate me. It is incredible that fifty years later I have found a use for them. Perhaps if I could have seen a reason for learning them then, I might have been more interested.

During the fifty years since the atom was split into its different components, scientists have made even more mind boggling discoveries regarding the make up of our world and the whole universe. Using mathematical formulae, a few enlightened scientists and mathematicians realized that it is quite feasible for other worlds, which vibrate at a faster rate than ours, to exist within the same space as our own.

Until quite recently it was thought that the speed of light was the fastest movement possible, but that is not necessarily true. Using our human senses that is an obvious assumption to make. It is not so long ago that it was considered impossible to break the sound barrier, but we are all now familiar with the supersonic boom. Our inability to experience something due to our human limitations does not mean that it does not exist. Such amazing energies have been found within the atom that what used to be looked upon as magic or trickery has become quite believable.

In the light of recent scientific discoveries more and more scientists and mathematicians are becoming convinced that it is possible for other worlds to exist. Planes of existence to which our etheric bodies and minds return when we leave physical life behind. There is such a wealth of information available from so many different sources that all the writers cannot be crooks and charlatans.

At this point I would suggest that anyone who wishes to study psychic phenomena from the scientific angle should read *Other Worlds*, by Paul Davies, and *Science of the God's* by David Ash and Peter Hewitt. In the latter the reader will find rational, scientific explanations for many of the subjects discussed in this book, such as spiritual healing and clairvoyance.

We now return to the seance room to find the connection between these two seemingly diverse subjects. To begin with, for those unfamiliar with spirit communication, I should explain what takes place at a materialization seance, using the power of a deeply entranced medium.

The sensitive usually sits in a cabinet or curtained off corner of the room. This is done so that there can be a build up of spiritual power, although I believe it is not always the case. The medium allows her Guides from Spirit to take over her physical body and after a few minutes she will fall asleep into a state of deep trance. From then on she is unaware of the amazing phenomena which take place in the room. The remainder of the group sit in a semi-circle facing the medium.

Ectoplasm issues from the nose and mouth of the entranced medium. Light has the effect of dissolving this substance so therefore every chink of light must be excluded. A low infra-red lamp is allowed so that the Spirit forms are visible. I have spoken to someone who has been able to embrace the materialized form of his father at one of these seances.

Solid objects are covered with luminous paint so that they are easily identified by members of the circle when moved about the room by returning souls from the etheric world. Metal cones are used to concentrate the sound of their voices and these can be seen moving through the air unaided.

There is a fascinating history behind this remarkable phenomenon of materialzation, going back to the 19th Century.

During that time there was a great deal of interest in every aspect of Spiritualism. Unfortunately the poverty of that era led some unscrupulous people to take advantage of grieving relatives and make money through fraud and conjuring tricks. To believe that all mediums are charlatans on this account is very short sighted, to say the least.

The exceptional talents of these remarkable people have caused them to be harassed and branded as frauds down through the ages, by a fearful, ignorant and insensitive section of society. Joan of Arc, who heard voices, suffered way back in the 15th Century.

In the days before films, radio, television and all the other modern entertainments with which we fill our leisure time there were a number of physical mediums. Dedication by the sensitive and members of the circle is vital for the development of all spiritual gifts, but particularly for this advanced form of communication. Consequently there are very few materialization mediums today. Some are practising their gift but do not make the fact known to the public because they are aware of the appalling treatment meted out to their predecessors. Although we have been connected with Spiritualism for fifteen years my husband and I have yet to have the opportunity of experiencing the amazing phenomena which occur at these seances.

Sir William Crookes and Sir Oliver Lodge, two eminent 19th Century scientists, were both knighted by Queen Victoria for their services to science. Independently they each made a study of materialization mediumhip because of the public interest in the subject. Although beginning their investigations as sceptics they each became convinced that their experiments showed that life continues on another plane of existence. It became apparent to both men and others, that in some way through the power generated by certain mediums, those in the etheric dimensions are able to slow down the rate at which their etheric body vibrates and materialize in the vibrations of our world.

Sir William Crookes experimented with many different mediums, but the work he did with Florence Cook convinced him that the sceptics were wrong. For over three years he was continually in the presence of Katie King, who manifested through the powers of Florence Cook. He was convinced beyond any doubt that Katie King and her medium were two separate beings.

Sir Oliver Lodge published two books recording the results of his experimentation entitled, *The Survival of Man* and *Ether and Reality*. Each of these highly respected scientists was sure that his findings would be verified in years to come and the secret proof lay within the atom.

From being feted as amazing physicists they were both labelled as 'cranks', once they published the results of their investigations into the continuity of life after death of the physical body.

Two of the most famous pre-war materialization mediums were Jack Webber and Helen Duncan. I shall devote the next chapter to their work in this field.

## CHAPTER THIRTEEN

Jack Webber passed into spirit life in March, 1940, after a very short illness, aged thirty-three. Although he died at such a comparatively young age, the last few years of his life were filled with demonstrating his remarkable gift to as many people as possible. He was a miner by trade, but he became so much in demand as a physical medium that he gave up his job in the pit to concentrate on his materialization mediumship.

Before the seance started Jack would be tied to his chair with ropes by people who were strangers to him and therefore had nothing to gain from fraud. The front of his jacket would be sewn up so that he could not get out of it. The power of his Guide, Black Cloud, was so great that he was able to dematerialize the jacket, leaving Jack still sitting in his chair bound by strong ropes, and the stitching of the jacket still in place. Photographs of this event are available.

Heavy tables would levitate on their own and move round while luminous trumpets would swoop around the room. Faces, which were about three quarters of life size would appear in the ectoplasm and the voices of the departed souls would be heard through a trumpet. Gradually whole forms would build with ectoplasm like a cowl over them. Hands would materialize and be felt by the sitters who said they could feel the difference between those of a man materializing and a woman.

His Guides were able to build so well that they could speak easily to the sitters, demonstrating that lungs and larynx must also materialize.

The amazing happenings at Jack Webher's seances were witnessed by many eminent sceptics of the time, including some from Fleet Street. Cassandra, a famous columnist from the *Daily Mirror*, finished the article recounting his visit with, "I went to scoff. But the laugh is sliding slowly round to the other side of my face."

One of our most famous and most persecuted of all physical mediums was Helen Duncan.

Helen was born in Callendar, Scotland, in 1895, and had a strict Presbyterian upbringing. Even as a child she heard spirit voices and was punished by her elders for repeating messages given to her psychically. She devoted her life to helping others and used her amazing gift to bring back loved ones to many hundreds of grieving relatives.

She was particularly busy during the Second World War when so many men and women lost their lives as a result of enemy action.

On one occasion a young sailor materialized giving information that he had gone down with his ship H.M.S. *Barham*. The news of the sinking of this vessel had not been made public and there was great consternation in high places when reports of what was transpiring at these seances filtered through to the intelligence services. Consequently, by devious means, some high ranking officials managed to attend one of Helen's seances and she was arrested for fraud. That is how, during one of the bloodiest wars in world history, a harmless medium was charged under the Witchcraft Act of 1735 and tried at the Old Bailey. Even Winston Churchill called for an enquiry and a reprimand was given to the Prosecution for wasting the time of the courts when the country was at war.

One of the charges levelled at her was that she swallowed yards of cheesecloth and by some miraculous means regurgitated it to form the ectoplasm. If it were not so serious one could only feel sorry for those displaying such pathetic, insensitive ignorance.

Helen Duncan was found guilty and sentenced to nine months in Holloway Prison. The only good to come from this whole charade was the eventual repeal of the archaic Witchcraft Act.

After her prison sentence she refused to give public demonstrations or allow any scientific research into her gift. However, in 1956 at a private seance, two unwelcome guests bluffed their way into the proceedings. As soon as Helen had gone into trance and her Guide had spoken, they grabbed her, flashing a white light. To be brought out of trance in this manner is devastating for a medium and she died thirty six days later from her injuries.

Is it surprising that today's physical mediums do not spread the news of their gift to the world at large.

I know of a physical medium now who has given up demonstrating her gift because she fears for her life. I tried unsuccessfully to get her to change her mind so that I could write from first hand experience. However, I have impeccable evidence from someone who was present at one of her seances when Helen Duncan returned to speak to her daughter Gena Brearly. Gena was convinced that for over an hour she was conversing with her mother.

Through the power of this same medium a little boy, who died from cancer in 1963, has returned and given the name and address of his parents. They have been reunited with him many times through this lady's mediumship and are in no doubt that they have been in the company of their son. I have spoken personally to this little boy's mother.

Raymond Lodge, the son of Sir Oliver Lodge, has materialized at these seances. He has donned a luminous jacket and boots and stamped around the room. He has banged himself with luminous drumsticks to demonstrate how solid he is.

Of course this all sounds quite unbelievable. That was the reaction when someone suggested that the world was round and not flat!

## CHAPTER FOURTEEN

Arguably the most controversial form of spiritual healing comes under the heading of Psychic Surgery.

It is performed in many different ways, but the healer is usually in a trance state, as described in previous chapters. The doctors from the 'other side' who carry out the operations while using the physical body of their medium, become as well known as their human instruments.

Mike and I were present at a healing session performed by Dr. Khan, who works through our friend Stephen Turoff.

Stephen is over six feet tall, broad shouldered and speaks with a London accent. That day, as we watched, he sat down as Stephen, closed his eyes and appeared to fall asleep. Three or four minutes later he stood up and introduced himself as Dr. Khan. His face, voice and bearing had visibly altered and he seemed to have shrunk. He walked across the room and asked me to roll up his trouser legs. As Dr. Khan he was shorter than Stephen and in danger of tripping over them.

In the room there was a couch for the patients and a table laid out with surgical instruments, cotton wool, a bowl of water, a small glass and a box of matches.

One patient suffering from cancer was told to lie on her stomach on the couch. Dr. Khan put a piece of flannel over her bare back and moved his hands about while diagnosing where he should do the surgery. All the time he was working he was quietly saying to the patient, "You will feel no pain." This phrase was repeated with each person he treated throughout the day.

He picked up one of the instruments, which I can only describe as a type of stiletto, and began to gently tap it into the patient's back, using another instrument. The patient did not flinch.

Removing the stiletto, he placed a piece of cotton wool, weighted down with a coin, over the wound. His assistant picked up the small glass, lit a match to burn the air inside it, and the glass was placed over the cotton wool.

A swelling gradually appeared inside the glass, and after about five minutes, when the swelling seemed almost to fill it, Dr. Khan removed the glass and scooped a liver-like substance into a bowl. He wiped away a drop of blood and a plaster was put over the small wound to keep it clear of the patient's clothing.

I am unable to report the results of this treatment, and describe it out of interest.

During the healing session Dr. Khan told us that there were about fifteen specialists in spirit working with him. On several occasions he seemed to take invisible instruments from invisible hands and appeared to be working on the etheric body. I was particularly surprised when he told one patient that she would need an injection. Dr. Khan went through all the motions of giving an injection with an invisible syringe and although the patient could not see what he was doing because she was lying face down, she visibly jerked when the invisible needle was put into her etheric 'bottom'!

Dr Khan also gave 'hands on healing' and asked Mike and I to join in to give extra power. He demonstrated to us how water changed into oil as he massaged it into a patient's skin. He scraped off the oil and showed tiny particles of calcium which had come away with it.

I cannot say that we saw miraculous, instantaneous healing that day, although one arthritis sufferer rang several hours later, while we were still there, to report that she was delighted with the improvement in her condition.

Stephen holds frequent clinics in Spain and many doctors have testified to the authenticity of Dr. Khan's work. His healings have been well documented.

During a television programme in 1992 I heard two people describe their experiences with Dr. Khan. They admitted they were sceptics when they first visited him and had gone for help with their conditions as a last resort when the medical profession had written them off. They each testified to the incredible healing which they had received from Dr Khan.

The following is an account written by one of our patients who also visited Dr. Khan.

"I came to the U.K. in 1985 after living in South Africa for forty years. The first year my health was perfect but then I seemed to pick up every virus around and was continually ill. My G.P. diagnosed M.E. (yuppie 'flu) and said there was nothing that could be done. He advised me to rest as much as possible. I was so fatigued all the time that I spent a great percentage of each day sleeping, in fact I wondered if I was going to die. To add to this hideous problem I developed extreme pain in my jaws, which absolutely nothing, not even the strongest painkillers could combat.

By now I realized that the medical profession could not help and I started to look for alternative treatment. Friends told me of two spiritual healers, Mike and Beth, who held regular clinics in Bath. Thus began a long programme of healing. After the first treatment I felt an immediate lift, and over the following months received much benefit.

About a year later I heard about Stephen Turoff who was purported to be a psychic surgeon as well as a healer. I felt motivated to visit him.

We were shown into a Sanctuary where I lay down. Stephen went into trance and seemed to be transformed into a shorter, German fellow by the name of Dr. Khan. He said there was a great deal wrong with me and he would operate. There were marks on my stomach and before leaving Dr. Khan said he would visit me during the night.

On the way home I said to me husband, 'I don't know whether to believe this or not'. I arrived home totally exhausted, put on a white track suit and went to sleep.

I awoke much later and decided to have a bath. As I was undressing I noticed that the waistband of the track suit was covered in blood. An injection mark was clearly visible above my hip bone and I realized that Dr. Khan had made his promised visit.

I was determined to have another session with Stephen Turoff (or Dr Khan) just to see if he would mention the injection. I did not say a word about it to Stephen when I went for my next treatment, but as soon as Dr. Khan came through he said, 'I came to visit and gave big injection'.

Between my yearly visits to Stephen Turoff and regular healing from Mike and Beth I am now painfree and feeling so much better. It once again feels good to be alive. Thank you to these wonderful, dedicated people and may God Bless them always."

One of the greatest psychic surgeons of all time was a Brazilian peasant affectionately known as Arigo. He was a most unwilling healer, being a devout Catholic.

A German, named Dr. Adolpho Fritz, who had died during the First World War, chose Arigo as his earthly instrument. He wished to carry on the work which he had begun during his lifetime.

When entranced by the spirit of Dr. Fritz this uneducated peasant would perform in seconds, without anaesthetic, the most complex operations, using nothing but an old penknife. He would plunge the knife into an eye to remove a cataract or into a stomach to cut away a cancer.

During the 1950's and 60's literally thousands of sick and dying people beat a path to his door. He would treat over three hundred patients in a morning and never accept even the price of a cup of coffee. Every type of operation was carried out causing no apparent pain or fear and with scarcely any loss of blood, even with the most serious conditions.

This almost illiterate man would write in German the most complex, unorthodox but effective prescriptions whilst in trance. Oddly enough, the strange mixtures recommended by Dr. Fritz did not work unless especially prescribed by him.

Arigo's healings were witnessed by many doctors and scientifically authenticated. There could be no question of sleight of hand or trickery because the miraculous results were there for all to see. He died in a motor accident in 1971.

I highly recommend to believers and disbelievers alike, John Fuller's book, *Arigo: Surgeon of the Rusty Knife*.

For some reason the country most renowned for its psychic surgeons is the Philippines. The gift has sometimes been handed down through generations.

In her book, *I Fly Out With Bright Colours*, Allegra Taylor describes graphically her investigations of the healers of the Philippines. The methods used are different from those of Arigo. The fingers only are used to part the flesh. It is a much more bloody business, but when the offending lumps of diseased tissue have been removed the body appears to close over, leaving no scar or just a faint red mark.

In a country of indescribable poverty, it is easy to see how tricksters and charlatans could cash in on this trade in human suffering. However, the 'proof of the pudding is in the eating', as we say, and there are thousands of people around the globe who will testify that they have been brought back from the brink of death by the powers of one of these amazingly gifted people.

It does seem that once a healer from the Philippines has been ' discovered' by

Westerners and transported to a European country for a few months with the lure of rich pickings, the God given power wanes.

This is a subject which will always cause great controversy and only personal experience and deep study will enable one to make up ones mind as to the authenticity of the phenomena.

I was interested in a quotation which Allegra Taylor made from a book which she bought in the Philippines entitled, *The Truth Behind Faith Healing in the Philippines*', by Jaime Licauco. In an attempt to offer a rational explanation he says, "What happens during a healing session involving psychic surgery goes beyond physical science and beyond the physical senses of man. Unless we change our fundamental assumptions regarding the nature of the physical universe and admit the existence of other levels of reality within which our healers act, then no explanation is possible or believable." Once again we are getting into the realms of 'other worlds' existing in the same space as our own, as I mentioned in a previous chapter.

No chapter on the subject of extraordinary healing powers would be complete without a mention of someone who was known during his lifetime as the Man of Miracles. His name was Edgar Cayce. He was born in the state of Kentucky, U.S.A. in 1877 and died in 1945.

Throughout his life he was a student of the Bible and a committed Christian. Like Arigo, who was to come many years later, he was a very unwilling servant of his gift.

As a boy he discovered that he could put himself to sleep with his head resting on his school books and awake knowing everything which they contained. This made him into a minor sensation with family and friends but it was the beginning of a life long problem of being 'different'.

The first indication of his extraordinary powers began during his schooldays when he fell into a coma after being hit by a baseball ball. He suddenly began to speak in a clear, authoritarian voice to his family gathered around the bed. 'I've had a shock from a baseball ball which struck my spine. The way to bring me out of this safely is to make a special poultice and put it at the base of my brain'. He named special herbs that were to be mixed with raw onion for the poultice. When no one moved he commanded, 'Hurry and get on with it if you don't want permanent brain damage'. After the instructions were carried out he fell into a deep normal sleep and by morning had completely recovered.

This was the first of many thousands of readings which he gave throughout his life whilst in a state of self hypnosis.

As his fame grew he was besieged by sick people, and some unscrupulous ones who tried to cash in on his gift. Whenever he tried to turn his back on the work which had been chosen for him against his will, he would lose the use of his voice. Strangely, this also happened to Arigo when he tried to disassociate himself from his powers.

On one occasion Cayce was thrilled to obtain a real job as an X-Ray photographer and thought he had broken free from his unwanted 'gift' at last. Unfortunately when the plates were developed patients were shown to have two spines, tails and various other peculiarities. His services were no longer required.

Under deep hypnosis Edgar would diagnose and prescribe the most incredible cures. When he awoke he remembered nothing that he had said. This was a source of great worry to him, in case he ever prescribed something which ended in a death. He never did. Not only was he able to give readings for people who visited him but he could also transport himself hundreds of miles away, to obtain information which he required.

One reading called for medicine no one had ever heard of. Under hypnosis Edgar named a chemist in Ohio who had one bottle left. The person named sent a telegram advising that the last bottle had been sold long ago. He put himself to sleep once more and the advice given was that one bottle had been overlooked and pushed to the back of a shelf behind a display of new products.

A second telegram was received saying, 'MEDICINE ON THE WAY, BUT HOW DID YOU KNOW IT WAS THERE'?

On another occasion a lady was prescribed something called 'Codiron'. Much investigation revealed no product of that name had ever been known. Edgar re-hypnotised himself and named a drug company in Chicago. The reply received from the drug company was one of bewilderment. 'HOW ON EARTH DID YOU LEARN OF CODIRON. IT IS A BRAND NEW PRODUCT, JUST PERFECTED. THE NAME WAS ONLY CHOSEN A FEW DAYS AGO'.

Time and again doctors tried to expose Cayce as a charlatan and a trickster, but they always ended up with 'egg on their faces'.

He moved on from medical diagnosis to give deeper help regarding the spiritual pathway and the pattern of the Universe. He referred to these as life readings.

Whilst in deep hypnotic trance he was told that reincarnation is a fact. Between incarnations the soul has access to all its accumulated knowledge and experience. It can choose for itself which body and which era will best help it to work out its own Karma. Once in the body such knowledge is erased from the conscious mind and retained only in the subconscious. Again we hear that reincarnation and the Law of Cause and Effect are at the root of our earthly existence. Remember this information was coming through an active lay worker of the Christian religion.

During another life reading the question was asked, 'Do planets have anything to do with the ruling of the destiny of man'? There was a strong reply in the affirmative.

At the Edgar Cayce Foundation in Virginia, they have vaults which house the thousands of records of the work of this amazing, yet humble healer.

## CHAPTER FIFTEEN

Running parallel with our healing work Mike and I have tried to help others find a meaning and purpose to their lives. We have collected an extensive library of spiritually orientated books covering every level of understanding. Anyone seeking a deeper knowledge may borrow them.

Seminars have been organised in our home. Twenty or more 'seekers of Truth' have squeezed into the lounge listening to philosophy or taking part in demonstrations of clairvoyance.

Occasionally, if a person shows genuine interest we take them along to a Spiritualist Church. We only take beginners when we know they will witness a high standard of mediumship. First impressions are very important in our opinion.

It must be understood that one finds some very gifted but some mediocre mediums working on Spiritualist rostrums. Each one has a gift, but some have developed their talent more than others. It is only by listening to a variety of clairvoyants as we did in the early days of our search, that one is able to make an assessment of the standard. There have been times when we have both said as we have left a meeting, that if it had been our first experience we would never have returned. So we always feel it is important for the first introduction to be impressive, as ours was, all those years ago.

Once we have shown the way, we feel that our job is done. It is up to individuals to pursue the interest for themselves. As we always point out, we are not evangelists or missionaries trying to convert others to our way to thinking. We merely show interested people where to begin and it is up to them if they wish to take up the challenge of further investigation.

Should anyone reading my words feel that they would like to visit a Spiritualist Church let me assure them there is no need to worry about going alone. There is nothing to be afraid of and you will always be given a warm, friendly welcome.

In my opening chapter I described the first service which I attended and most churches follow a similar format. Part of the proceedings will be given over to clairvoyance or giving proof of survival as it is called. Do not be worried about this. If the medium speaks to you, all you have to do is to say clearly either 'Yes' or 'No', which ever is appropriate. Mediums do not mind if you say 'No', when they offer information which you cannot understand. Often the event or the matter referred to will be remembered afterwards, when you are going over it in your mind.

Do not be afraid that any private matters will be spoken of in public. Everything will be put in such a way that only you will understand the underlying meaning of the message.

Another part of the service will be a spirit inspired address by the medium. We hear about vicars working on their sermons all day Saturday, ready for their Sunday services, but a person working on a Spiritualist platform may not know the subject of her talk before she stands up to give it. She tunes in mentally to the spirit vibrations and her Guide impresses her mind with words of wisdom. Most people in the congregation find there is something in the philosophy which appears to be especially directed at their own situation at that time. I have frequently found this to be so.

I must again emphasise that there is nothing to be afraid of and you will not be brainwashed or roped in to join anything against your will.

When Mike and I discovered the world of spirit communication, we felt we wanted to rush out and tell everyone. It seemed incredible that this had all been going on throughout our lives and yet we had only just discovered it.

Naturally, when we first started visiting Spiritualist meetings the one person I wanted irrefutable evidence from was my brother who had been killed in the flying accident so many years previously. We had heard proof of survival which could be accepted both by us and other people, but never anything that I could say without a shadow of doubt, "That information definitely came from my brother."

After several years of hoping I became very disheartened when nothing was forthcoming. One day while walking my dog and thinking deeply as usual, I thought, "I might just as well give up expecting to hear from Laurie, he has obviously moved on to other things". No one else knew that I had come to that conclusion.

The following week we were at a meeting and during the session of clairvoyance the medium said to me, "I've got your Mother here", and he proceeded to describe her.

I replied, "I'm sorry I don't remember my mother, she died when I was young."

"Did your mother have any brothers?" he asked.

I answered, " Yes, several."

After concentrating for a moment the medium said, "Wait a minute, it's not her brother, it's your brother she has brought here, you've got a brother in Spirit. He is saying that you had given up hope of ever hearing from him!"

As you might imagine this sent quite a thrill through me and the medium finished by saying, "The number forty-five should be significant in this connection".

I thought about this message long and hard, but as far as I was concerned the number forty-five had no significance for our family.

The next morning I was busy doing my ironing, pondering on the information of the previous evening, when I decided to search through a small box in which I keep a few family treasures. I store letters in it written by my mother to an Aunt, before I was born. I wondered if perhaps the family was living at No. 45 at that time and I had never heard about it.

No, that was not the answer. Then I picked up the last Christmas card which my brother had sent to me. I had always kept it amongst my treasures, but had not looked at it for years. It was a normal service type Christmas card with a photograph of a Beaufighter in it. That was the type of aircraft he was flying when he was killed.

Staring me in the face beneath the photograph were the words No. 45 Squadron.

For me that evidence was very special.

During 1992 I had an unexpected sitting with a medium whom I did not know. After she had been talking about various members of my family she asked if I had any questions I would like to ask. There had been no mention of my brother and I just said, "Well I do have a brother in Spirit." That was all I said.

After a few seconds she said, "I can see him now with his fair, wavy hair. He is telling me he was here one minute and gone the next. That's funny I can see a lot of blue sky around him and he is saying he is back up there again now, and you will understand what he means."

Of course I realized that he was referring to his life as a pilot.

As far as the medium knew, he might have been drowned at the age of twelve, had a long lingering death from cancer at the age of forty or committed suicide even at the age fifty. For me personally, that was very good evidence that she was in touch with him.

Although one can read and listen to overwhelming evidence received by other people, it is necessary to search for one's own special proof. You cannot be fully convinced by second-hand information, however many books you read or Spiritualist mediums you listen to during church services. Do not be disappointed if you do not find convincing personal evidence straight away. Keep searching and have patience. Eventually you will find your own golden nugget of proof that will convince you alone. It may be something seemingly quite trivial to another person but for you it will be priceless.

As time goes on the type of communication received alters. After all, once you are convinced that life really does continue, but in a changed environment, there is no point in being given more of the same information.

Gradually the spirit world will start to give advice on your spiritual problems and the path which you should be following, as happened to me in May, 1985.

My husband and I were present at a demonstration given by the gifted clairvoyant Doris Collins in the Bristol Hippodrome. The theatre was full to over flowing, which meant there were many hundreds of eager people hoping for a message from their departed loved ones.

As soon as she started her clairvoyance Doris picked out Mike and myself from this huge assembly.

She straightaway mentioned the fact that we are healers, and then she said to me, "You are a teacher, and you are retiring". This information really astounded me as I had only decided that week to give up work and I had not given in my notice. She went on to say, "But you will not be giving up teaching, you will continue to teach for Spirit." Presumably this volume is part of their plan for my retirement years!

As one develops ones psychic gifts and draws closer to the spirit realms a heightened awareness becomes apparent.

Suddenly you know something but you do not know how you 'know'.

I can best illustrate this from my own experience.

As we progressed with our healing development I began to find myself sure of things having happened without being physically informed.

In 1985, we were on a coach holiday in Yugoslavia when I 'knew' there was something wrong with our beloved boxer dog, Sam. The coach journey home took three days and all the time I could not rid myself of a feeling of foreboding. Mike dismissed my worries because Sam had been perfectly well when we left.

As our home came into view at the end of the journey I was telling myself that in two minutes I would know how foolish I had been. Unfortunately my 'knowing' had been correct and Sam had been put to sleep that day because he was in such pain.

On a number of occasions I have told my husband that someone associated with us had passed into spirit. The same feeling comes over me that I had all those years ago when my brother had been killed in Malaya. I even felt it when the lovely dog 'Truus' passed over. Sometimes, we have had a phone call within half an hour verifying what I have felt so strongly. Of course, this does not happen every time, but if I suddenly feel depressed for no reason, I start wondering who it could be.

When we set up our healing centre at home, I 'knew' that we had to also have a library. Spreading spiritual knowledge was to be an important part of our work. Some people just come to the house to avail themselves of the books and discuss general spiritual matters.

On another occasion, in 1984, we went to Cardiff to have private sittings with a medium who had been recommended to us, named Paula Wood. After we had returned home and were discussing Paula's good mediumship I 'knew' that I had to invite her to work in our Sanctuary.

I rang immediately and she gladly accepted the offer.

She had only recently given up her post as a nurse to become a professional medium. Her Guides had told her not to worry and everything would be taken care of. They told her she would be working in Bristol, but as she had no connections here she could not understand how it would happen.

They also told her she would be working overseas and now America, New Zealand and Iceland are regularly on her itinerary.

Sam, our boxer dog always had to investigate everything which went on in the house. When Paula was giving readings in the Sanctuary he was always hanging around outside. On one occasion he managed to push the door open and joyfully bounded in only to be hastily bundled out again. On Paula's first visit, after he had passed into Spirit, she said, "I couldn't keep Sam out today, he's been in there with me all day."

If the spirit world want something to happen then events will be made to fall into place to ensure that it does. I have no doubts at all that I was impressed to invite Paula here to work in our Sanctuary. Since 1984 she has visited several times each year to give private readings.

There is so much emotion in our house on those days when people are given undeniable proof that their loved ones are communicating with them through Paula. So many leave with tears of joy streaming down their cheeks.

They are given seemingly trivial pieces of information which to the recipients are overwhelming evidence.

For example, one young women told me after her sitting that Paula was told to mention a bottle of boiled water.

To the rest of us that would mean nothing at all, but it brought tears to the eyes of the recipient of the message. Her grandmother, to whom she was very close, had sworn by boiled water as a cure for everything. She never came to visit without it and it was a family joke.

That is a good illustration to all aspiring mediums that they must give everything which comes to them, however odd it may seem.

## CHAPTER SIXTEEN

Much has been said and written about the foolishness of young people playing with ouija boards. I thoroughly endorse everything and further wish to emphasise that it should never be practised alone at any age.

Should anyone have no experience of this form of spirit communication the following is a brief description.

The letters of the alphabet are placed in a circle on a polished surface, and the words 'yes' and 'no' are put inside the circle. Many questions asked can be answered by either 'yes' or 'no', so this is done in order to cut down on the spelling. Commercially made boards also have numbers on them, again to shorten the amount of movement involved.

A small glass is placed in the centre of the board and the members of the circle each lightly rest one finger on it.

My own introduction to this was as a nineteen year old student at training college, when a crowd of my friends decided to 'have a go'. I remember it was agreed beforehand that no mention would be made of forthcoming examinations, in case anyone was told they were going to fail!

When someone who considered herself knowledgeable on this subject began by saying, 'Spirit of the glass, are you there?' I was convulsed with laughter. The serious members of the group bundled me out of the room and I was banished from the proceedings thereafter.

No one would have persuaded me then that it wasn't 'a load of rubbish'. I was very firmly entrenched in the material world at that time in my life. Of course now, over forty years later my ideas have changed totally.

However, I reinforce my earlier remarks, young people should not dabble, and no one should practise it alone, whatever their age. There is great danger of becoming obsessed.

A young lad aged about fourteen, who had been foolish enough to play with a board on his own, was brought to our home by his elder sister asking for help to exorcise him. He had come under the influence of the spirit of a 14th Century sailor who had been murdered. It began as a joke, but very soon the lad found this lost soul had attached himself to him and was influencing his everyday life. The spirit made contact through our board, gave us his name and we were able to send him on his way.

Young people are particularly vulnerable to this kind of problem, because they open themselves up psychically, with no protection from their own Guides.

On the other hand, under the control of mature adults the ouija board is an excellent means of communication, provided the motive for using it is correct. My reason for saying this will be made clear later.

In 1983 we were asked by a friend if we could help an acquaintance of hers to get rid of a 'presence' in her house.

Articles had been lost and found in strange places, while some had actually been thrown around in the attic.

Since we had no experience of this type of phenomena my husband mentioned it to Jack, a friend of ours, whom we knew had been investigating spiritual matters for a great number of years.

Jack suggested we should all gather at the house with an ouija board and try to contact this unwelcome spirit.

On the agreed evening there were six of us present including the owners of the house and their seventeen year old son.

We opened the meeting with a hymn, followed by a prayer asking for the protection of the members of the circle.

Each person present placed a finger on the glass, and it soon became apparent that the glass was being moved by someone other than the six of us sitting around the table.

We asked the name of the soul who was communicating, and the glass spelt out *Bill*. We asked how he had died and he spelt out *accident*. In reply to the question, 'Where did the accident take place'? the glass spelt out *mine*.

This was quite a feasible answer because our meeting was taking place in an area of Bristol where there had been old mine workings. We told Bill to look for a light around him and he would find his loved ones who were tryings to reach him.

The glass whizzed around the board saying, *thank you, thank you.*

We could feel the joy of this lost soul being expressed through the movement of the glass.

This type of communication is known as Rescue Work.

As far as I know there was no further trouble and an unpleasant feeling in the house disappeared.

Several months later Jean and Frank, in whose house we had had the sitting, came to us for healing. Thus our paths crossed again and after a long chat on all spiritual matters, we decided to meet once more in their home.

On the evening of 11th January, 1985, we began what was to be several years of awe inspiring contact with an intelligence greater than our own, on the spirit side of life.

The point I must make very clear at the outset is that this situation was set up by those in spirit and not ourselves. We demonstrated at the beginning that our purpose was to help 'a lost soul', and no selfish or foolish motives were involved. Therefore we proved to those on the spirit side that we were suitable candidates for the work which had to be done.

I am aware that a concept such as my last statement is very difficult to assimilate. It is only when one has been studying these matters for many years that it is possible to take for granted, as we do, that there are outside forces guiding our lives.

The spirit side had worked towards gathering a group of people together who would not be motivated by personal gain.

They needed contacts on our side of life who would learn from the experience, make good use of the knowledge which was to be imparted and pass it on to others.

In writing this book now I am carrying out part of the reason why we were so privileged to have been chosen.

Before the second meting I was checking through my Scrabble letters which we were to use, when I discovered the letter 'J' was missing. The thought came into my mind that I had better improvise in case anyone named John wished to communicate.

As soon as we had sung our hymn, prayed for protection and linked with the glass, it was apparent that we had contacted someone. The only way I can explain the situation is by saying that the glass seems to come alive and glides round the letters.

We asked the name of the person who was with us and we received the reply *I am known as Brother John*. (Thank goodness I checked on the 'J' I thought).

Over the following months and years we came to know Brother John as a truly wonderful friend. We always knew when we were linked with him because he would begin with what we referred to as his call sign, '*God bless you all*'. His departure and the close of the session was always indicated by the lovely Latin phrase *pax vobiscum* (Peace be with you).

The only time I remember he did not begin with those words was after we had had a break for several months and his first words were, '*at last*'.

Brother John was the spokesman for a number of highly evolved souls in spirit and he told us they were known as the Inner Group of Brothers of Light. I believe they are also the group known as the 'White Brotherhood'.

On the first evening in which we made contact with Brother John and his Group, we were used for rescue work.

Someone named Charlotte took control of the glass and we were all amazed at the joy and emotion we could feel as the glass whizzed around spelling *thank you*, when we had pointed her towards the light. We were able to help someone who said he was *William* and also someone calling herself *Aggie*.

We were all rather feeling our way on that first evening, so we decided to meet again the following month as Brother John had told us that there was a great need for rescue workers.

On the 8th February, we met again in the same house. Before we opened the session Frank had been telling us about some Germans that he had been entertaining all week, as part of his job.

We began the sitting in our usual way and then the following words came through. *To you all love* followed by *To work. We are gathering power. You have been entertaining my countrymen in your city.*

We asked if Brother John was a German and the answer was *no. Ja ja nein*. We then realized that we were no longer talking to Brother John and asked if we were speaking with a German.

The name *Oscar* was spelled and we asked how he had died. *The war* was the answer. Jack then took over the conversation and told him to remember his family and look for the light.

*Thank you* was spelled and we realized Brother John was in charge again when *he has gone* was communicated.

Then followed a collection of letters which I thought was jibberish. They were *nowotny*.

Suddenly, Mike recognised with great joy that the letters spelt the name of a

German fighter pilot for whom he had a great admiration. Mike spoke to him and referred to his stand against Hitler over the massacre of British prisoners of war. Nowotny replied *it was my duty*.

When we asked why he had come to join our circle he replied *We are helping you. That is the purpose.*

We asked if there were any others they wished us to help on their way and he answered *they have been listening*. We realized that through our work with Oscar we had been able to help many other lost souls. Nowotny said *we are always watching for helpers*.

After a moment the glass began to move very slowly, and we knew we were in touch with another lost spirit.

We asked if he knew his name and we received *no* followed by *guns fire mud*. From this reply we deduced that we were in contact with someone who had been connected with the First World War. We asked if he was German, British, French or Belgian, but each time the answer was *no*, then he spelt *Polish*.

We asked if he knew his name but he spelt *no* followed by *Ypres Somme*. When we asked him if he was alone he replied *mist*. I said 'Were you a Catholic?' to which he answered *yes where is heaven*.

Jack explained that he was not alone and to look for a light through the mist. Then he seemed to remember his name and spelt *Viktor*, followed by *farewell*.

We were chatting amongst ourselves about the incredible things which were happening when Brother John took control again and said, *You are still amazed.*

Mike was making a joke with Jean about having a cup of tea and I told him he would get told off for not being serious. Straightaway the answer was *we like humour*.

After about half an hour we resumed contact with the board. Brother John took control and said, *We too come for refreshment. We are prepared to answer your questions. You have been asking several times in recent days now the opportunity is here.*

We asked about rescue work and further work for Spirit. Then Mike asked if there was anyone close to us with them and the reply was *many but we do not encourage because they become earthbound.*

We asked why Walter Nowotny had come to talk to us and the reply was *why don't you ask him.*

We had not realized he was still there, but then it became apparent that he is part of the group working with us. Nowotny said *we are all brothers. The link has taken a long time to establish. It was not by chance.* We asked if he knew we were all going to be there and the reply was *that is not always possible to tell. We may not dictate.*

He was then asked about his time in the German Air Force. Nowotny replied *that was only one life.* We asked him to tell us about his life in Spirit and he said *what purpose would it serve. There are halls of learning.*

Brother John finished the evening by saying *now we close in love may the great spirit bless you all.* We then closed with a prayer and each one of us felt drained of energy.

To say that we all had food for thought would be an understatement and we decided to meet again the following month.

## CHAPTER SEVENTEEN

On the evening of Friday, 8th March, 1985, Mike, Jack and myself once more joined Jean and Frank in their home, hoping to be of use to our wonderful friends on the spirit side of life. We began by singing the 23rd Psalm, followed by a prayer and a few minutes meditation.

As soon as we made contact with the glass it spelt out, *We would seek your help. We want a period of quiet.*

For the next quarter of an hour we all sat and meditated, during which time my hands were charged with healing energy. When we linked with the glass again Brother John spelt out, *Thank you. We have made contact with a group in flight to your city. Ad Astra.*

I recalled that before we left home I had seen on the Television News a report that a young Englishwoman had contracted Lassa Fever while working in Sierra Leone. She was being flown home by the R.A.F. which would account for the Ad Astra quotation from the Air Force motto.

When I asked Brother John if this was the case to which he was referring, he replied, *Yes. Sick person on board.*

We asked if there was anything else we could do to help and the reply was, *It was done.*

One of the group suggested that those of us who are spiritual healers were used and the answer came back as follows, *You are all needed, It has been the subject of much prayer. She is a beautiful soul. Her family has been most anxious. Prayer is coming from all her helpers on both sides. We needed help via yourselves.*

Brother John also gave us the correct time that the plane would be landing at Bristol Airport. Later while talking amongst ourselves and trying to fathom out why we had been chosen to help, the glass spelt out, *You are essential because you are aware.*

Needless to say, we followed the progress of this young lady's recovery very closely through the press reports. It was very thrilling several weeks later to read that she was well enough to leave hospital.

When this interesting episode was over we asked Brother John if there were any other souls who wished to make contact with us. The board replied, *We have many here who would like to speak, you are able to speak with them. Veritas vintas crede et verde.*

We were astonished to find ourselves being spoken to in Latin. My own schoolgirl knowledge of the language had been long forgotten and when we asked Brother John why we were being spoken to in this manner, he replied, *Because you are thinking you are infallible.*

In our excitement we had been 'jumping the gun' and guessing the endings of words incorrectly, before they had finished spelling. They decided to calm us down by communicating in Latin!

The next communicator began by saying, *I was much in harmony with your opening hymn, (Psalm 23).*

We asked if we were still with Brother John and the answer was *No. I was a prelate of the church.* We asked his name and he replied, *Laud William.* The question 'To which church were you connected'? was answered by the word *Canterbury.*

Some of us vaguely remembered hearing about Archbishop William Laud in our school history lessons, and we asked him the date of his birth. He replied 1573. We received quite a shock when the date of his death was given as 1645 followed by the word *Beheaded*!

We asked who had succeeded him as Archbishop and he said he did not know. I spoke and referred to him as Archbishop, to which he replied, *Please there are no titles in heaven. Primus inter pares.* We believed this last Latin quotation to mean, First among equals.

This was followed by, *To teach the problems of life we are now making contact for the future. Vade bene. Now rest you are in need.*

During our break we were discussing Jean and Frank's problems regarding spiritual development, and when we linked again with the glass we received the following communication, *There is too much anxious thought about salvation. Why do you trouble. There is a way for each to go. The masters eagerly wait for those who are linked to them by ancient wisdom. You prepare by meditation. Meditation has to be carefully set to achieve its objective.*

*When a wise teacher walks among you and can see your inner state help will be at hand. We give the key when we say be harmless in thought, word and deed. So easy to say, but difficult to do.*

We asked the purpose of meditation and the reply was, *That you can learn and use your mind. You have spent previous lives in the devotional.*

We asked where this took place and the answer was, *We think either as monk or nun in the Middle East or in a Monastery in Tibet.*

Mike enquired if there was any procedure we should follow when doing our rescue work. *You should at all times send our love and talk as you are doing. Prayer is useful*, was the reply.

Mike's knee, which had been damaged many years previously was giving a great deal of pain so I enquired if it was possible for him to receive healing for the condition. The reply was, *It is karma Mike. All becomes clear. We are grateful for all you do.*

We closed with a prayer.

Needless to say, the first thing I did on reaching home was to scour my encyclopedia for details of the life of William Laud.

The entry was exactly as it had been given to us. Laud William, 1573-1645. Became Archbishop in 1633. Tried for treason, sent to the Tower and was beheaded.

Mike and I have since been to Canterbury and discovered that after William Laud there was a gap of fifteen years when there was no Archbishop.

I have gone into great detail regarding these communications because I wanted to convey the incredible standard of the link which we had with the world of Spirit.

After an evening such as I have just described I would feel completely drained and sleep solidly for about nine hours.

Unfortunately, the couple in whose house we had been meeting, were unable to handle the incredible communications which we were receiving. They began to imagine that somehow we were influencing what was happening. To what end? We were just as astounded as they were!

We did not meet in that house again.

## CHAPTER EIGHTEEN

Early in 1986 Mike and I discussed with Jack and another interested friend Pam, the idea of setting up an ouija board circle in our own home. We wanted to find out if it was possible for Brother John and his group to contact us in a different venue from where the first link was made.

The previous year, soon after the first exciting contact, we had shared our experiences with a group of relatives who all wanted to take part in the same fantastic link with spirit.

A meeting was arranged in our home and about ten of us crowded around the table expecting a marvellous, instant spiritual experience.

Absolutely nothing happened. The glass did not shift. That disappointment taught us a great deal. We realized that our wonderful link was something special and not meant as a spectacle for all and sundry to witness.

So, on the arranged evening the four of us, Jack, Pam, Mike and myself gathered round the table and followed the usual procedure. We sang a hymn to raise the vibrations, asked for protection through prayer, read our absent healing list and then meditated for about ten minutes. During the meditation we each tried to clear our minds of material problems.

Our diligence was rewarded. The glass spelled *God bless you all*, and we knew we were once again in touch with our beloved Brother John. Pam was welcomed to the circle and we just seemed to carry on from where we had left off at our last communication.

We met weekly and some months later two others, Anna and Joan were allowed to join us. I say 'allowed' because unless those working on the Spirit side are able to blend with our auras, contact will not be possible.

Once we asked if two young women could come along as observers but we received an emphatic *No*. We were told that they would bring too much apprehension with them, which would impair the link. Brother John made it quite clear that the choice was ours, but we would receive no answer from their side.

As I mentioned earlier, one of the reasons for the setting up of the group was for the purpose of 'rescue work'. This was not an easy task by any means. At times we felt at a loss to know how to help, when the contacting souls were so muddled. Sometimes it would take half an hour of gentle questioning before an entity with whom we were linked could understand that they were physically dead and in spirit. It would take still more time then to persuade them to think of their loved ones and look for the light.

With hindsight one wishes that more comprehensive notes had been kept of the proceedings which took place over the next few years. So much happened that it would be impossible to recount everything. I've picked out some of the most interesting episodes although to us everything received is of great value.

Many times we have received pleas such as *Please help me. Please help me.* Once we were able to help a young woman calling herself Juana. She told us she had been a cook on the ship, the *Belgrano*. The *Belgrano* was an Argentinean vessel sunk during the Falklands War. We have not been able to check this, but I mention it for interest.

On one occasion a member of the group asked for the title of a book which would help her sister understand the meaning of life.

First of all we were given the name *Annie Wilson*. That's an old fashioned name I thought, it must be going to be something written in Victorian times. Then the word *Holford* was spelled, which was recognized as a place in Somerset.

The title of the book was given as *The Wise Virgin*. None of us had ever heard of this book and then the most amazing communication took place.

*Wait a moment* was spelled, followed by a pause of about thirty seconds. The board we were using had numbers on it and the glass pointed to 301 followed by the word *Decimal 41*.

When one of the group asked for this book at the library, we discovered that we had been given the exact class number which was stamped in the front! It had been written in *Holford*, but I was amazed to see that the publishing date was 1979.

The book is about five women who overcame life's problems to find their own pathway and their own awareness of who they really are. It is a very deep book in my view, and I would not recommend it for a beginner.

Some months later we had teaching about the importance of meditation, and how it is the basis of all spiritual work. One of the group asked Brother John if he could suggest a book on the subject.

The title given to us was *The Yoga Sutras of Pantanjali*. Not one of us had any knowledge of that worthy volume. Sure enough when one of the group asked for it, a copy was unearthed from the depths of the Bristol Central Library!

I mentioned earlier in the book that there are mediums known as psychic artists.

Mike and I had visited one about a year before we were contacting spirit through the Board, and we secretly thought the drawings given to us were rubbish.

Mike's was the drawing of a scholarly looking gent with glasses on the end of his nose. It meant nothing to either of us. However, we kept the sketch, and one night after the session with the Board, we showed the drawing to the rest of the group, as an example of psychic artistry.

The next week, as soon as we linked with the glass we received *You saw my portrait last week. Parlez vous Francais?* We asked the name of the communicator and the glass spelt *Dr. Charles Henri Monet du Salvan*. I asked if Salvan was his surname, to which he replied *My mother's name*. I believe it is the practise in France to tack on the mother's maiden name.

During the meditation, before linking with the glass, Mike had 'seen' an old leather bag. The doctor confirmed that it was his leather bag. He had been a Herbalist and he would use the bag when he was out collecting his herbs. He told us that he is a member of our healing team, specializing in nervous complaints. When we asked him if the drawing was a good likeness, he replied, *Only fair not fit to hang in the Lycee.*

*The drawing by psychic artist Peter Hammond of Dr. Charles Henri Monet du Salvan, a member of our healing team who first made contact with us in 1987. At his request this picture now hangs in our Sanctuary.*

That really taught us not to be too hasty with our judgement of other people's mediumship.

Dr. Charles has been through a number of times over the years but in June, 1993, he challenged us with the words *"Why is my picture hidden?"* We apologised and promised to frame it. (How did he know that after six years the drawing was still in the drawer and had not been destroyed?) The portrait was duly given pride of place on the Sanctuary wall and on 18th July he greeted us with the words *c'est magnifique*. We could all feel his pleasure and he made some remark about being hung in the Louvre. During that session we quizzed him about his life on earth. He confirmed that he had been here during the last century. He explained how he had used leeches for bleeding and purging. Then he turned his attention to Jack, who had had a heart attack some months before, with the words *now Jack mon cher rub your little finger to abate heart palpitations*. We asked if he had any other tips and he replied *press big toes for cramp and circulation*. He then referred to his Chinese friends who use these methods and we assumed he meant acupuncture and acupressure. At one of our remarks he came through with that favourite French phrase *sacre bleu*, leaving us in no doubt as to his nationality in that life.

On 1st March, 1992, we were able to be used for an exceptionally rewarding 'rescue'. We had invited a Dutch friend Toni to join the circle and Brother John greeted her with the words *you bring the aura of the low countries. She will explain to you about peace*. We then had a discussion about the Peace Palace in The Hague.

After a while we were aware that someone new had taken over the glass. It was obvious from the way he answered our questions that he did not realize he was dead. He spelled *these do gooders have robbed me blind*. We didn't find out who they were, but we learnt that his name was *digger* and he had lived in South Africa at some time. When Pam tried to explain to him that he was in Spirit he came back with the words *what is spirit*.

When he heard Toni speak he remarked about her accent and Jim suggested he might speak in Afrikaans. He replied *no*, but then added *dankie* and *totsin*. We did not understand but Toni did. We learnt that he had been all over the world with the Navy and Jim suggested that in times of danger at sea he had probably prayed to God. He agreed that he had done so and Jim told him to do it again. Suddenly the glass whizzed around saying *I can see my mates I am free, free*. That really was a wonderful moment when we could feel our success with another 'lost soul'.

Two months later Digger linked with us again and said *can you help us we are trying to rescue a cobber. He is in the northern territory. He thinks he is on earth*. We were told that the lost soul's name was Ginger Spence. When Jim mentioned his name he spelled *Who is that*. Mike explained to him who we were and tried to make him realize that he was no longer on earth. He also told him that his friend Digger was no longer on earth and trying to contact him. He replied *You dinkum. I'll do you if it is not dinkum. Let me think. There's an old native here with me and he says we are in the dream time but I don't believe him*. We continued to take it in turns to explain to him that the information he was receiving from us and the native was correct. He replied with *I don't believe him, never did believe the crazy natives. I see, touch, hear. What about my gold. It's here I can touch it.*

We realized his attachment to his 'poke' of gold, as he put it, was keeping him earthbound. From careful, lengthy questioning we learnt that he had been a gold miner in the Northern Territory. He told us he had left Newcastle Waters, New South Wales with his stake in 1929. He told us he would be 65 in 1930. We told him his mate Digger wanted to talk to him. Ginger said *Digger can you hear me?* Digger spelled *Ginger listen to Mike*. Mike asked if he could see a light yet. *No but the native has gone. Where's my gold?*

We could gradually feel the truth dawning on him and he said *at last I see the dawn. I can now understand. I died of thirst and have been dreaming. There was a storm and I lost all my animals. Hold hard who is that lady. I see a lovely lady and Digger. Oh boy, oh boy, I can't believe it.*

That brought a very satisfying evening's work to a close.

## CHAPTER NINETEEN

During the years of our privileged association with Brother John and his Group we have had much splendid teaching on the subject of 'life' and also the 'afterlife'. We have also questioned him deeply about 'where he is' and how he is able to communicate with us.

We understand that when we sit in our circle round the board a light goes out into the spirit world and many souls are attracted to it. Brother John has described it as rather like a huge amphitheatre with tiers of seats stretching upwards, with our small group below, in the middle. One communicating soul whom we rescued said she thought we were playing bridge! Those in the Astral plane gather to hear the teachings which we are receiving from the more highly evolved ones who are communicating with us. We find it difficult to believe that some of us still on earth are more knowledgeable about spirit life than those already over there!

It is wrong to assume that when a person moves into Spirit they suddenly become all-knowing angels. We are exactly the same as we were in the body. Nobody goes to heaven and sits around strumming a harp all day waiting for 'God'. We have had lost souls asking us time after time *Where is Heaven?* This is particularly the case when people have been brainwashed by a certain religion while on earth.

For most of us our transition into spirit appears to be easy, and we are met by our loved ones who have gone before us and are eagerly awaiting our arrival. However, for some reason which we do not know, there are souls who get lost and find themselves in a 'mist' – that is how they have explained it to us during our 'rescue work'. Those who have a strong emotional attachment to something in the physical world, such as Ginger Spence and his gold, or who have a fanatical belief or hatred of something appear to have difficulty.

One evening, after a particularly deep teachings session regarding, as we would say, the set-up on the other side, I was instructed by Brother John to draw a diagram. I was told to put seven marks, equally spaced on a vertical line and then the words were given to us, as shown below.

*Divine*
*Monadic*
*Spiritual*
*Intuitional*
*Mental*
*Astral or emotional*
*Physical.*

When the word Monadic was spelt, we had some difficulty, since none of us knew the word. *The Oxford Dictionary* explains a Monad as an ultimate being, and Monadic as the first of a series. We took it to mean that when we reach that state of being, we would be at one with the Divine Source.

However, I don't think anyone reading this need worry too much about the Monadic level, as I for one, will no doubt still be in the Astral when I return to Spirit next time.

The diagram sets out what souls are ultimately striving for. We come back to earth many times in order to learn lessons and thus gradually purify our spiritual selves.

Each time we hold a circle we are just hoping we shall be successful, since we are not guaranteed anything. Over the years we have learned what we can do to help the link.

I insist that once I have arranged the room we do not go in there until we are ready for the sitting. When the members of the circle arrive they are shown into another room, where general news and chit chat can take place. However, as time has gone on we have found that what we discuss before the session often influences the evenings communications. Therefore, if there is a problem or a particular question we would like answered we bring it up in our conversation before we sit at the table.

The timing also has to be correct. We normally sat at 6 o'clock, but one Christmas I suggested to the others that we change it to 4 o'clock, so that we could have a little party afterwards. My big mistake was not asking 'the other side' if it was all right to do this. On the appointed day we sat down at 4 o'clock and the first thing that was spelt was *Please delay for two hours*. When the two hours were up and we asked the reason for the delay they said *Delay due to conjunction of the planets!* There is just so much we will never understand until we are on the other side.

We have also discovered that it is vital that we sit in the same places. Once we decided to change the seating arrangements and they spelled *Leave at once*. When we asked what was wrong they said *The order*. When we were back in our original places the meeting went ahead unhindered.

We understand that to protect us from any unwanted influences they put a protective etheric cover over us during the proceedings. They have told us that sometimes they have had to fight for control if there is any unexpected outburst from anyone. Once we were told that there had been a tear in the protective covering when something unexpected happened. So we have learnt to keep excitement and conversation between ourselves to the minimum.

At one point Jack, who had been in the circle since its formation was seriously ill for several months and unable to attend. Mike, Pam and I went through all the procedures diligently on several occasions but we were unable to make the contact. Later, Brother John told us that they had to have the four of us to make the link. It was while discussing Jack's serious illness and the healing which we know he received that Brother John said *None of you need fear coming to our world it is beautiful beyond the telling*, which I think is a lovely comforting phrase.

In the unseen world there is a library known as the Akashic Record in which everything that has ever happened is recorded. That is a concept very difficult for those of us with finite minds to digest. However, from the Akashic Record Brother John has obtained information about our previous lives. Mike and Jack had been Brothers Dominicos and Tristos, members of the Orders of Brown Monks and Black Monks whose monastery had been at Stoke's Croft in Bristol during the 13th Century. Mike had worked in the Herborium, growing herbs for healing purposes and Jack had been keeper of the records of chantries, which was to do with the singing of masses. Years later we were given an extra interesting snippet of information regarding the Black Monks. Their habits were not really black only blue-black because blackberries were used to dye the material.

The three women of the group had been members of the Little Sisters of the Poor at Frome Gate Priory in Bristol. It was a source of amusement when we were told that I was Sister Benedicte, Mother Superior. Even in that life I was a 'bossy boots'. There have been several references to my being a Nun. Once Mike saw clairvoyantly a beautiful church and we were told that he had seen my church which was the Church of the Sacred Heart in Constantinople, but it is no longer standing.

Of course one can argue that there is no way of proving those facts, although we believe implicitly what is given to us by Brother John. However, in April, 1993, I was told about a lady in Gloucester who performs what she calls Past Life Therapy, which sounded 'right up my street'!

Her name is Gaye Wright, and we got on very well. I purposely told her absolutely nothing about myself before the therapy, because I did not want her to be influenced in any way at all. She was happy to go along with this.

She put her hands on my head and tuned in to the three Chinese Guides who relay the information to her. I could not believe my ears when she kept saying, "I keep seeing you in religious orders. When I ask for a specific life to tell you about I get more about self sufficiency and the monastic life. You appear to have spent many lives in this manner searching for the Truth about Life"! Although this time I have turned my back on organized religion I am still seeking the Truth about Life. It also explains the incredible fascination I have always had about Nuns and convent life. I am drawn to any book or television programme on the subject. I had imagined that everyone was interested in what went on in 'closed orders', but I find that it not the case.

For me that confirmation of my 'doings' in past lives was overwhelming evidence of the continuity of life.

## CHAPTER TWENTY

During the Summer of 1986, I was fortunate to spend a week at Stanstead Hall, in Essex. This lovely old building, in its own grounds, was donated to the Spiritualist Movement by one of its pioneers, Sir Arthur Findlay.

To visit Stanstead is a unique, unforgettable experience. To be in the company of so many people from around the world, all of whom know, without reservation that the spirit world is a fact, brings great satisfaction and stimulation.

From my arrival on Saturday until the following Wednesday I did not read a newspaper of see a television set. Every minute was taken up with engrossing topics to discuss and lectures to attend.

By the Wednesday afternoon I felt I had reached Spiritual Saturation, and decided not to attend the afternoon lecture.

However, this was not to be.

While relaxing in the lounge before lunch, I struck up a conversation with a lady who had come especially to hear the afternoon's lecture. It was being given by a friend of hers, but she could not tell me on what subject the lady was to speak.

I felt a strange compulsion to change my mind, and found myself sitting in the lecture room almost against my wishes.

I could not get interested in the talk, because the person giving it was German and her strong accent made the content of what she was saying difficult to follow. It was something to do with a new form of spirit communication taking place in Brazil. No one could really understand what she was trying to convey to us. People at the back were sneaking out, but as I was at the front I had to stay put.

Then I heard the lecturer mention something about seven levels of consciousness. My mind flew back to the diagram which I had drawn for Brother John a few weeks previously, and I 'knew' that what I was listening to had some connection with our group in spirit.

She mentioned contacts of hers living in Brazil who were given advanced philosophy from the spirit realms.

I began to take more interest and was fascinated when she spoke of herself and a medium friend being in touch with a highly evolved group, known as the White Brotherhood. To let them know that they were around, the Group would send a white feather for them.

On one occasion she was visiting the Pyramids in Egypt, when a white feather came fluttering down, much to the consternation of the Guide, since no bird had been in there for three thousand years!

I left the lecture hall knowing that what I had been trying to understand all afternoon, had a significance for me, but I did not know what it was.

The Circle met at home during my absence and when I rang, later that evening, I was told that Brother John had said I would have something interesting to tell them on my return. I ' knew' then that somehow my visit to Stanstead was connected with that day's lecture.

I also ' knew' that I was being impressed to seek out the lady who had given the lecture and talk to her about our Group, and Brother John.

The next morning I managed to speak to her alone for a few minutes, and gave her a brief outline of our activities. Her name was Gretchen and she was very interested in what I was telling her. We arranged to meet later in the day for further discussions.

That afternoon I decided to walk alone to the nearest village. I really did need a change of atmosphere by then.

My route back to the Hall led me through a small area of woodland. As I was walking along, deep in thought, I looked down, and there, right by the toe of my shoe was a White Feather! I cannot explain all the different emotions which surged through me at that moment. There was not a bird in sight, let alone a white one.

I scooped up the feather, wrapped it in a tissue and put it in my pocket.

I was bubbling over with excitement, and when I met Gretchen later that evening, the first words I said to her were, "Guess what I found in the wood this afternoon".

She immediately said, "A white feather."

After that we talked in depth about our communications with Spirit and I told her that if ever she was in Bristol she should come and visit us.

On the morning that we were to leave, I got up early and dressed. I was about to make coffee for my room mates when just by the window I found another white feather. I could swear it had not been there when I had first got out of bed.

At breakfast I told Gretchen about my latest find and she was delighted. "Now I know why I was impressed to give the lecture this year. I gave the same lecture two years ago but no one was interested."

A few days after I returned home I received a telephone call from Gretchen to say that she would like to take me up on my offer to visit Bristol, while she was still in England.

We held a special Circle for her to attend, and she was reunited through the Board with her best friend. This friend was German, and much of her communication that night came through in that language. Gretchen was given a great deal of encouragement from Spirit, and was thanked for the work she is doing towards spreading spiritual knowledge.

One phrase which I wrote down was *Nach best en krafften*. She told us that the English translation is, 'Do the best you can'. The German words were followed by the English words *Put two dots over the a*. No one in our group knew the language, so this lesson in German punctuation was good evidence that nothing was coming from any of us. The communication ended with the English words *It is a high calling to which all your feet are directed.*

I felt very honoured to have been chosen by the highly evolved workers in

Spirit to act as their go-between and bring Gretchen in contact with those for whom she has been beavering away so long.

My thoughts now return to a holiday which Mike and I had in Tossa da Mar in Spain.

Before we went, we mentioned to Brother John that we would not be meeting the following week. He replied, *Go to the local church and offer a prayer for the world. Light a candle in the faith. The name will surprise you. Here they are laughing.*

We could not think what our friends in Spirit could find so funny.

However, we found the local church and did as we were asked. We lit a candle, a most unusual practise for us, and said a prayer. We then tried to find out the name of the church.

As neither of us spoke any Spanish, and the name did not seem to appear anywhere, we were unable to carry out this part of the request.

On our return we explained the situation to Brother John and he told us that the name of the church was, *Juan de Los Angles*, which when translated means John of the Angels! That was what was causing the mirth on the 'other side'.

I recall another story which might cause a few raised eyebrows.

Joan, one of the group, worked in an office in the heart of old Bristol, an area steeped in history.

Mike arranged to pick her up outside the building at 6.45 p.m. to bring her to our home for the Circle.

She became so engrossed in her work, that when the time came for her to pack up, she found everyone had gone home and she was locked in.

The next ten minutes were spent chasing through the building from the basement upwards, trying to find a way out. She eventually found the caretaker on the ninth floor, and he then took her right down to the basement again to open a door down there.

The first soul to communicate that evening said, *I was whispering to you tonight!*

From much painstaking questioning we gathered that he had been with Joan during her frantic search to find a way out of the old building. We learned that he had been *Gentry* and he had been a *Freebooter* at the time of the Bristol Rebellion.

We asked if he had had a friend while he was on earth and he spelt *Clover*.

We then found a lady named *Clover* was in control of the glass. She told us that she had come to Bristol from Westminster Docks, and had supplied *Victuals and slops for ships*. We asked if she knew the soul who was communicating with us and she said she always referred to him as *Toff*. We learnt that he was a deserter and she had taken care of him. In the end he had been discovered and to use her words, *Was run through with a broadsword*.

Our conversation with these two entities lasted one and a quarter hours, but we were eventually able to bring them together again.

The most amusing outcome of this story is, that on the Monday morning when Joan happened to pass the caretaker in the corridor of the building where she worked, he said, "You know, I hate having to go down to that basement, I always think there is a ghost down there."

If he only knew!

This truly remarkable link which we have is an on-going experience and each time we meet we learn something new about what inevitably lies in store for each and every one of us. The stories are endless but this must surely be enough for the most ardent sceptic to be going on with.

## CHAPTER TWENTY-ONE

Mike and I always go to great lengths never to bring any religious bias into our healing work. The curative powers of our helpers in Spirit are for everyone, whatever Creed they may follow.

One day in 1988, I took a phone call from an elderly lady who was making enquiries about our work. I could tell from her voice that she was no longer a young woman.

"Is it Spiritual Healing?", she asked, with what seemed to me a strange emphasis on the word 'Spiritual'. I replied in the affirmative and then she said, (almost reluctantly it sounded to me on the other end of the phone), "My sister and I would like to come along."

The appointment was made for 2.30 p.m. the following day. We were able to do this, because by that time both Mike and I had taken early retirement, in order to devote more time to our healing work.

Over lunch I said to Mike, "We must be very careful not to mention Spiritualism this afternoon. I think we have a couple of elderly Christians coming and we don't want to upset them."

As they walked into the lounge to sit down, one of them turned to us and said, "This is my sister Mary, she is a Trance Medium!"

To say that we were flabbergasted, is an understatement, especially when recalling my words over the lunch table.

This was one occasion when my sixth sense was definitely switched off.

We learned that they were two widowed sisters living together for company. They had had their own trance circle in Wales for many years, before coming to Bristol. A gentleman who came to help with the gardening had told them about us.

About seven years previously, we had had our garden landscaped by this same gentleman. When we paid the bill, I had given him one of our business cards even though he knew nothing about spiritual healing.

All those years later, he was chatting to the two ladies when the subject of healing came up. He remembered the card and gave them our phone number.

I never cease to be amazed at how those in Spirit arrange things for us.

When you meet people who are on the same wavelength as yourselves the conversation just flows naturally. That is how it was with our new friends, Mary and her sister Betty. We spent most of the afternoon swopping stories of spiritual experiences. After the healing we made arrangements to see them again the following week.

Before we began on the second occasion Mary said, "Don't bring me round too quickly at the end, as I seem to go very deep during the healing."

When we had finished and I was about to gently speak to her, there was suddenly a loud voice booming out saying, "Greetings, it is good to speak with you". We were astounded to hear this in place of Mary's usual soft, Welsh tones. It was her Guide, Grey Eagle speaking to us.

Since then we have been privileged to hear his words of wisdom many times.

Before long the four of us decided to set up a home circle in our bungalow. The purpose of the circle was to be further development of our healing powers. It was only after we had made these arrangements that I remembered some information that we had received three years earlier through the mediumship of our friend Paula Wood. She had told us, during a special sitting with her, that sometime in the future we would have the opportunity of having our own circle with a medium.

During our meetings we all meditated for half an hour, allowing our helpers to draw close to us. In this way we made ourselves better channels for the healing power. Afterwards we mentioned anything we may have seen clairvoyantly or sensed in any way. I often felt unseen hands gently touching my face.

By speaking of our experiences we let our helpers know that they were succeeding in their efforts to communicate with us.

On one occasion Mary said to my husband, "Do you know anything about a person whose face is drawn up at the side. I felt someone very close and they put that condition on me."

Both Mike and I were amazed to hear this.

For several months during our healing sessions, Mike had attracted my attention and pointed to the side of his face. It would be pulled right up at the side and beyond his control. Once the healing was finished, the entity who had taken over would withdraw, and his face would gradually return to normal.

Later, when Mary went into light trance, the helper who had this facial condition when he was on earth, spoke through her, and told us that his name was Thomas. He said that he had been a doctor when he was last in the physical body and deals with power for general healing. On another occasion we were spoken to by Robert, who said he dealt with eye conditions.

During our meditation one evening, I clairvoyantly 'saw' a beautiful oriental girl, who appeared to be travelling in a carriage, and at the same time the song 'I am Siamese if you please', was going through my head. Later, when Mary was in trance, a sweet, gentle voice spoke to me. She told me that I had 'seen' her, and she was one of my Guides. I was told to call her Singalong, because like me she enjoyed singing. I am always singing around the house, and we attract to us souls of like mind. Her voice, when she speaks to me through Mary, is in complete contrast to the booming tones of Grey Eagle.

Many entities have come through from the higher realms to speak with us. They have given us great encouragement, and told us of the far reaching effects which our work has had in the world.

Normally we did not have contact with our loved ones in Spirit. That was not the function of the circle. It was purely for the advancement of our healing work. However, on one memorable occasion my own mother was allowed to speak to me. We were both so overcome with emotion that she had to withdraw because tears were streaming down the medium's face.

Once again, those people reading this who have never witnessed trance mediumship will find the events which I have described difficult to visualize. Search for yourselves is my advice and you will be surprised what will unfold for you.

## CHAPTER TWENTY-TWO

While thumbing through the many diaries which I have kept since we began our spiritual search, I have come across accounts of a number of experiences which to some people would come under the heading of 'spooky'. However, I think many will find them interesting.

The first one happened to me on Sunday, 2nd June, 1978, only seven months after we had become aware of spiritual matters.

I decided to go to my favourite Spiritualist Church that morning because I knew the demonstrating medium was one whose work I held in high regard.

As I sat listening to the beautiful, meaningful words of her philosophy I became aware that I was looking at, or being looked at by a face from the world of spirit.

Forming next to the medium were white eyes, white mouth, black top hat, black jacket and a white shirt with a ruff down the front. It reminded me of someone dressed up for the Black and White Minstrel Show.

I closed my eyes and opened them again. The apparition was still there.

This form was visible to me many times during the service at different places around the medium. I sat there quite mesmerized and couldn't wait to rush home and share the experience with Mike.

I must point out that there was nothing frightening about this, just exciting.

After the first appearance, whenever I was at a service given by that particular medium, (and only that one) the same amazing apparition would show itself.

After seeing him on at least six occasions in different churches, I eventually explained to the medium after the service what had been happening. She immediately said, "How lovely, you must have seen my father. When he was on earth he would dress like that and provide entertainment in the Somerset villages. You must have been tuning into our vibration."

That was really a remarkable experience so early on in my search. Oddly enough, although I have attended this lady's services many times since then, he has never shown himself to me again.

One evening in 1980 we were sitting in a home circle run by a friend, when Mike was given his first example of clairvoyance. We were in a darkened room, with our eyes closed, meditating. Afterwards he described what he had seen. Right in front of him was a bush. It was so clear that he could see every vein on every leaf clearly. When something is seen clairvoyantly it is the clarity of the picture which distinguishes it from imagination. Since that first illustration of clairvoyance my husband has 'seen' many interesting things, but one incident stands out in our minds particularly.

We were meditating in the same home circle and afterwards he said, "I saw a long wooden building with a verandah – the type seen abroad in hot countries. Suddenly it burst into flames. Then I seemed to be looking down between my feet at something which looked like bushes with wispy spirals of smoke coming up from them."

We all tried to give interpretations of what he could have been seeing, but nothing we said could possibly have been anywhere near the truth.

This took place during the troubles in Rhodesia in the early 'eighties'. One evening we were watching the six o'clock news on television, when a long wooden building came up on the screen and Mike exclaimed, "Look, that's the bunglow I saw, in a minute it will burst into flames!" A moment later it did just that. The next shot showed a number of spirals of smoke coming up from the ground. We realized that the pictures were being taken from a helicopter. The fires he had seen between his feet were way below him.

We have never been able to work out how this incredible phenomenon occurred. Those pictures had been taken over the Rhodesian countryside and by some inexplicable means, Mike had tuned into the events here in Bristol, presumably at the time they were taking place.

I am reminded of another' strange incident involving television.

A drama serial about the French Resistance during the war entitled 'Wish Me Luck' was being shown. My husband was in the room with me, but not watching.

The episode was coming to an exciting climax. The camera zoomed in on a young English girl sitting high up in a barn, using a wireless transmitter. The producer was making the most of a nail-biting situation when suddenly I became aware of a young women in white standing in the foreground. She had dark hair, dark eyes and was dressed in a long tunic or a sari, without the head piece.

A quiver of excitement ran through me. I expected the English girl to be caught red-handed with her transmitter. The figure in white crept along behind a low hedge looking across at the girl and I was thinking, "What on earth is someone dressed like that doing in the middle of the French countryside, during the war."

The scene faded, bringing the episode to an end. I sat thinking and felt sure there was something strange about what I had been watching. I waited impatiently for the next instalment which was to be screened the following week.

The scene began again with the English girl and her transmitter in the barn. Of the 'figure in white' there was never another sign!

I know the story sounds far fetched but this definitely happened to me when I was completely wide awake. Even now I can remember the thrill of excitement I felt when she appeared on the scene, expecting the heroine to be caught. I am not one of these people who gets totally absorbed in dramas I see on television and start imagining that the characters and story lines are true. I can offer no explanation, except to say "I definitely did not dream it."

I have often wondered if anyone else saw this 'extra' figure on the screen or even if the camera crew were aware of any strange phenomena during the filming of the scene.

I recall a medium saying to me once when I was picked out for a message during a church service, "I am getting a connection with Australia. In a few days you will receive a letter with some good news."

I have a very close friend in Australia, but we only correspond about twice a year, at the most. I was not expecting a letter at least until Christmas, which was four months away.

Sure enough, five days later there was a letter on the door mat, with news that she was hoping to come to England the following year.

The letter was dated the day on which I had been given the information. She had been on holiday and decided to drop me a line.

My last teaching post involved a great deal of driving. One afternoon I was travelling along when suddenly I 'knew' I was going to have a puncture. A few minutes later I felt the familiar bump, bump, which indicates a flat tyre. This particular piece of spookiness occurred before we had any knowledge of these matters and I was so unnerved by the experience that I had to return home.

A similar event happened many years ago while I was living in Singapore, but I have never forgotten it.

As I left a cinema with a friend to make my way back to the car park, I felt convinced that I was going to find a flat tyre. Sure enough, there is was. A very 'odd' feeling came over me, but I kept that particular piece of spookiness to myself, in case people thought I was mad!

I recall waking up one morning in 1983, to find my room flooded with dancing golden lights. I hastily shut my eyes again, not being sure what was happening. I re-opened them and the lights were still there. After about three minutes they gradually faded away and the room was back to normal.

A few weeks later a medium in a church said to me, "I am being told that you have seen spirit lights."

I had guessed what it was but it was reassuring to receive confirmation.

We have had other experiences which don't really come under the heading of 'spooky', but I think some readers may find them of interest.

For instance, once while visiting a psychic fair we decided to 'have a go' at the Kirlian photography stand. Kirlian was a Russian scientist who invented a camera which could photograph the energy field around human beings. For convenience the hands are used.

The end result is an x-ray type photograph showing black wisps coming from the fingers. Experts in the field can read health conditions and other psychic information from these photographs.

When ours were printed everyone on the stand gathered to look. Our hands did not show just wisps of black, they looked as though they were covered in black hair. The gentleman in charge who was American said, "Gee, what a couple of power houses we've got here. How are you using all this energy?" We were pleased to be able to tell him that we were spiritual healers.

That leads me to another interesting phenomenon. On occasions, when I am looking at a particularly spiritual person, I am able to tune in and see the Aura or energy field around them. Every living thing has an aura, and I think most mediums have this ability. In my experience, the more spiritual the person, the stronger the aura. I usually describe it as being like the 'Ready-Brek' advert. There is a shimmering light all round the person, but more strongly visible around the head.

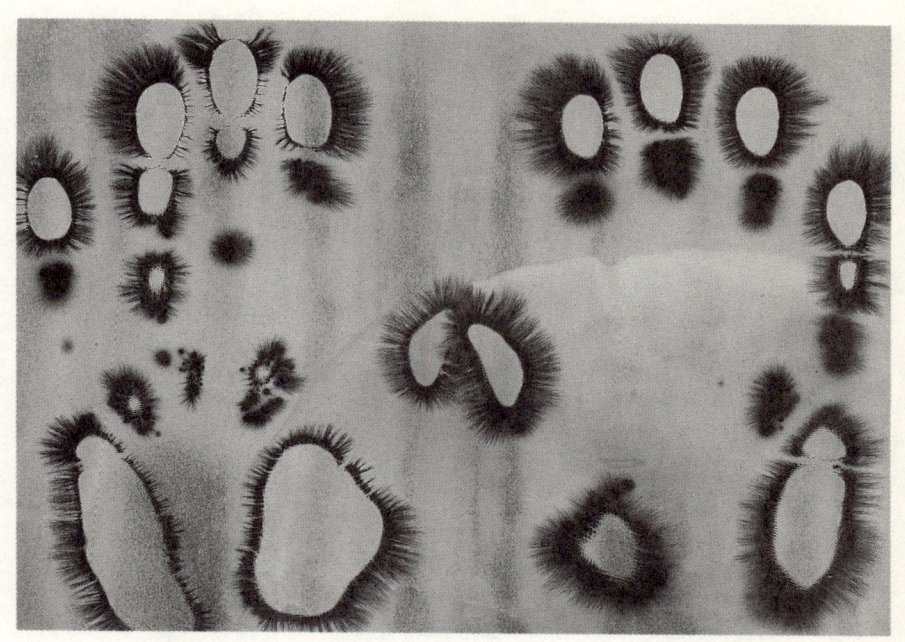

*Kirlian Photography – healing energy emanating from Mike's hands.*

When I put my hands on a patient's head for healing, it feels as though they are resting on a spongy cushion. I am aware of the energy field around that person.

Some mediums and healers are able to see colours in the aura, and use this for diagnosing health conditions. If the physical body is diseased, then the 'life force' is weakened, manifesting as a muddy-coloured aura.

When I speak of a person who is spiritual, I mean someone who is sensitive to the needs of others, generous with their time, unselfish and willing to 'serve' in what ever capacity necessary.

Spirituality has nothing to do with singing in the church choir on Sunday or calling oneself a 'Born Again Christian'!

## CHAPTER TWENTY-THREE

No doubt interested persons who have read this far through my story have labelled me a Spiritualist. That is far from the Truth. I do not consider myself affiliated to any type of church or organization. I am extremely grateful to the Spiritualist Church for all the knowledge I have gleaned from attending their services. There is no better place for anyone seeking the truth to begin their search.

I consider myself a 'free-thinker'. My interest goes beyond the confines of any man-made form of worship. There is a whole universe and parallel universes, the whereabouts of which I want to discover.

To me, it appears that all religions have grasped one facet of the diamond of truth and built up their own ideology around it.

I know that for some people participation in the set rituals of an established religion gives a sense of security, a feeling of continuity and a 'belonging'. This is especially true for those who were born into a family where the tenets of a specific belief were strickly adhered to.

I also realize that the Church provides a focal point in the lives of many families and communities. Much good work is done and support is given in many ways.

Unfortunately many souls cling to beliefs which were chosen for them by their parents who, in turn had been brainwashed by their parents into believing that everything taught by the Church was the truth. Religions place human beings in pigeon holes and keep them there through fear. It appears to be a mortal sin to even consider there might be an alternative pathway of thought. We only have to consider the atrocities which have been perpetrated in Northern Ireland over the past twenty years to understand the veracity of that statement. I was appalled to hear a Catholic child on television say that until she went to America for a holiday with a group of children from all areas of the Province she had never spoken to a Protestant child. She even seemed amazed that Protestants were normal children like her Catholic friends.

This chapter is not aimed at those who are comfortable with their beliefs. I am attempting to clarify the situation, as I see it, for the many thousands who can find no solace or answers to their questions from the teachings of the established religions.

What seems to have been overlooked by the orthodox churches is the fact that it is the *message* and not the *messenger* which is important. Jesus was a highly evolved soul who incarnated to bring his message of *love*, not to have millions of people falling down on their knees before him. The Commandment given to Moses which says, *love thy neighbour*, encompasses all the rest. If everyone on earth lived by that *message* and loved everybody, (even beetles, as my small friend said) there would be no more wars or bloodshed in the name of the various man-made religions.

If you have an enquiring mind, perhaps you are asking, "Why have I never heard or seen anything on my television about an alternative way of looking at life? Why have I never seen a service from a Spiritualist Church, with mediums, instead of men dressed up wearing dog-collars?"

The answer is quite simple. The fundamentalists of the orthodox churches have a stranglehold on the religious programmes departments of the mass media. After all, where would their jobs and those of all the clergy go if everyone knew that life goes on, regardless of what they believe and there is no need to be afraid of dying'? One Sunday morning I watched one of these mealy-mouthed religious mouthpieces showing the viewers all the religious newspapers which are published each week. No mention was made of *Psychic News*, even though the Spiritualist Church is now a recognised religion.

Conjurors who earn their living through sleight of hand and trickery are allowed to have programmes in which they can spend as much time as they wish denigrating the work of genuine mediums and healers. Anyone trying to put forward the case for rational thinking and logical truth without the trappings of religion, doesn't stand a chance of getting their message across the airwaves. A friend of mine has spent twenty years trying to break down barriers, in an effort to be given the opportunity to put forward on television the case of the physicists and rationalists, as regards the truth of 'life after death'.

Shirley Maclaine, the American film actress, has written a book entitled, *Out on a Limb*, which I highly recommend. She tells the story of her own introduction to spiritual matters and her subsequent investigations into the deeper meanings of this life and previous lives. She was interviewed on television by a chat-show presenter, and I was appalled at his tongue-in cheek, smirking, condescending attitude towards her. This man, who had been brainwashed by the Catholic Church since the day he opened his eyes in this incarnation, had the nerve to treat this intelligent woman as a joke. Her knowledge had been gained by personal research and investigation over many years. She had not soaked up religious trivia, which had been fed to her by others, like a piece of blotting paper.

On another occasion, an agony-aunt of the television received a letter from a woman who had lost her nearest and dearest and was unable to come to terms with her loss. She was asking the so-called expert if she thought going to a medium would help her. Straightaway this television personality said it would do no good whatsoever. She gave her a metaphorical pat on the head with such words as 'time is a great healer'.

These attitudes should not be allowed on national television unless, of course, differing views are afforded an equal amount of time.

Although the Christian religion preaches 'life after death', the clergy appear to be terrified of the truth actually being demonstrated to their flock. Proving to the man-in-the-street that death is nothing to be afraid of is looked upon as consorting with the Devil, (whoever he might be). Demonstrating to souls, desolate with grief, that their loved ones are indeed still close at hand, just on a different plane of existence, appears not to be tolerated at any price.

The brainwashed young people who call themselves 'Born Again Christians' are a fine example of this. They demonstrate outside Spiritualist meetings against something of which they are completely ignorant. They are merely mouthing doctrines which have been handed down for centuries.

Do they ever stop to think of the multi-millions who have been tortured and slaughtered down through the ages, in the name of their man-made religion? What happened to Jesus' message of *love*?

Their Church was established at the Council of Nicea in AD 325, by a few power hungry priests. The gold vestments, ridiculous hats, rituals and incantations were designed to fill uneducated peasants with awe and fear. It was a way of keeping the rabble in check and power in the hands of a chosen, educated minority. In my submission, the established Church has held sway over the lives of the rest of us for far too long. As we progress towards the 21st Century, at a time of compulsory education for all, everyone should have the facts of 'life' put before them, not the outdated shibboleths of our forefathers.

The whole fabric of our society appears to built around belief in Christianity. I recall, many years ago sayings to a young teacher who was applying to become a headmaster, "I'll never be able to apply for a headship, because I couldn't stand up in front of the children taking services." He replied, "You don't have to believe in it, you just go through the motions." I find the hypocracy of it all, quite overwhelming.

Why should children in this day and age be taught to have faith in something for which they are given no rational explanation. Education is supposed to train young minds to work things out for themselves and come to their own satisfactory conclusions. To search for an answer to the most important question they will ever ask, i.e. "What happens to me when I die?" is forbidden them.

In the 1990's fewer that 15% of children are church goers. Those figures speak for themselves. The hierarchy of the Church are completely out of touch with today's youth. Proof, evidence and the fundamental reason for why they are here, is what they are seeking. If the compulsory teaching of Christianity in our schools was doing any good, then the churches would be full every Sunday.

No-one is being asked to give up their religion or form of worship. Those who think as I do, feel that everyone has the right to have the true facts put before them, the opportunity to satisfy their curiosity and the freedom to make up their own minds.

The belief in the Catholic and High Church of England religions that one can go before a man, confess ones sins and be forgiven, is quite preposterous. Those are man-made rules, not God-made. Every human soul is responsible for his/her own wrong doing. No other man, however high up the ecumenical ladder he has managed to clamber, can wash away someone elses 'sins' The Law of Cause and Effect is absolute, throughout the whole of creation. Everything we do, good or bad will be balanced out one day, in future incarnations if not in this one.

During the years when I found it impossible to believe in the God which the churches portray, I had terrible feelings of 'guilt'. Everyone around me seemed to be content to swallow everything that had been drummed into them since childhood. I felt very isolated.

'God' is not an old man up in the sky, of whom we must all be afraid. 'God' is love and the 'life force' within every living thing, from which we may all draw strength.

What right do Christian missionaries have to take their Gospel to other parts of the world and instill their fear of 'God' in the minds of others? Human beings who have been happy in their own philosophy, freedom of thought and worship for thousands of years have been indoctrinated by them. It is as though the religion of the 'white man' must be superior to that of the coloured races. What nonsense!

Since I have been studying spiritual matters from many different angles I have been able to look at the Bible in a different light. Before my eyes were opened to the real Truth, I dismissed the whole book as a load of fairy tales. I can now equate the writings to my new found knowledge.

The stories which immediately spring to mind are those which recount Jesus' healing miracles. When he put out his hand and cured the blind man, the man 'sick of the palsey' and all the others chronicled in the New Testament, I am able to believe that it really did happen. The same power is channelled through Mike and myself when we give healing. The difference is, Jesus was a highly evolved soul and therefore a much purer channel for the healing energies than we are, or ever likely to be in this incarnation.

When Moses went up into the mountains and wrote down the Ten Commandments, I am sure he was spoken to clairaudiently. Highly evolved souls in spirit wished to convey those guide lines for correct human behaviour.

I know it is possible for an entity to materialize at a seance, therefore I am quite prepared to believe that a highly evolved soul such as Jesus could do likewise in front of his disciples after his death.

I now understand that the Bible is part of what is known as the Ancient Wisdom. Writings which have been given to man from Spirit and handed down through the ages.

However, all these accounts were written many years after the events occurred. They were re-told and re-translated from several languages before reaching our modern English Bible. Much of the teaching is abstract and obscure and it is up to individuals to make their own interpretations. Distortion of the facts is inevitable and it is puerile to imagine that everything within the Bible is true.

The world has been in existence for millions of years, while Christianity has been in operation for a mere two thousand years. Is it likely then, that God has only been concerned about the human race for that short amount of time?

God is *love*, and that power has been at work in the world since the beginning of time. Every so often, down through the ages, a highly evolved soul has come back to earth to teach the true spiritual values. Jesus was one of these teachers, as were Krishna and Buddha.

In India today there is another holy man named Sai Baba who can perform all the miracles attributed to Jesus and more. I shall talk about this 'living God' in my next chapter.

## CHAPTER TWENTY-FOUR

No book on the subject of Truth would be complete without a mention of Sri Sathya Sai Baba. 'Sathya' when translated from the Hindi means 'Truth'.

Sai Baba is an Avatar who lives in India. 'Avatar' is a sanskrit word meaning 'an incarnation of God on earth'.

Sai Baba is revered by millions of his countrymen and women. Although comparatively unknown in the west, thousands of his devotees from around the world fly into Bangalore each year to pay homage and to be in his presence.

When I write of his devotees do not imagine the bead bedecked hippies of the 'sixties', searching for a guru. Among Sai Baba's followers are scientists, professors, lawyers, teachers, politicians, engineers, doctors, shopkeepers, housewives and taxi-drivers.

Sai Baba was born at sunrise on 23rd November, 1926, in a small Southern Indian village, named Puttaparthi, about a hundred and fifteen miles from Bangalore. A large Ashram (sanctuary) has been set up there, where his followers gather. Another has been founded at Whitefields only fifteen miles from Bangalore, known also as Brindavan. Sai Baba spends most of his time at these two Ashrams although he does travel to Bombay and other Indian cities.

This is Sai Baba's second incarnation. His first began in India in 1872 when he was known as Sai Baba of Shirdi. During that 'life' he performed healing miracles and gave spiritual teachings to his followers. Before his passing in 1918 he foretold his rebirth, which would be eight years hence. Sai Baba has now said that he will pass in the year 2020 and reincarnate a few years later, being known as Prema Sai. He has named the village in which he will be born. That life will take him on into the 22nd Century.

A visit to his Ashram is an unforgettable experience. There is a large compound in front of the main temple where he lives and the devotees gather morning and evening for what is known as 'darshan'. At these times Baba will emerge, dressed in an orange, floor length robe. He is short and slight of figure with a mass of black bushy hair framing his benevolent face. He moves slowly along the rows of his patiently meditating visitors, twenty-five thousand multi-racial devotees is quite a normal gathering, and there are often many thousands more.

One of the miracles performed by him almost daily is the materialization from his finger tips of a grey, scented ash called vibhuti, which he drops into the cupped hands of delighted recipients. Vibhuti has special healing properties and it has been known to appear on photographs of him in various parts of the world.

In March, 1992, I was amazed to read an article in the *Daily Telegraph* entitled, *How the Ashes came to Harrow*. The writer was reporting the appearance of vibhuti on pictures of Sai Baba in a small house in Harrow.

*Sri Sathya Sai Baba – AVATAR.*

The owner of the house, a devout Hindu, but not a devotee of Sai Baba, had built an extension to his house in 1988 in order to have room for a snooker table. Following Hindu custom he built a shrine in the corner of the room and invited about fifty friends to the opening ceremony. Some of the visitors were Sai Baba devotees, who sang bhajans, which are devotional songs. During the singing, coconuts which had been placed on the shrine as offerings, split open. A highly fragrant nectar flowed out of them. Then an image of Sai Baba, lightly dusted with vibhuti, appeared on a second coconut. Gradually this room has become a place of pilgrimage for thousands of people of every faith, not just devotees of Sai Baba. There are images of Christ, Buddha and symbols of the Muslim faith alongside pictures of Sai Baba. Vibhuti has appeared on all of them. The owner of the house is as surprised as anyone. A researcher from London University said, 'I saw ash appearing on the photograph as I sat in front of it, and I have no doubt that the phenomenon is genuine'.

To return to the 'darshan' lines at the Ashram in India. Many who sit patiently waiting for Baba to appear are hoping to be healed, while others wish to hand him personal letters or messages from devotees in foreign countries who are unable to be there in person. A lucky few are called into the main building for a personal interview. Most are content just to be in his presence and receive his blessing. All those who have been privileged in this way say they feel themselves engulfed in an ocean of love and compassion. When he looks into their eyes it is as though he knows everything about their innermost selves.

Sai Baba's message to the world is simply *love*. God is *love* and Sai Baba is the embodiment of it. *Love* in this sense means service to all mankind. This service must be a natural urge from within; there should be no sense of duty attached to it. In his words, "Duty without love is deplorable, duty with love is good, love without duty is divine." He puts it another way which appeals to me even more. He says, "Hands which help are holier than lips which pray."

Throughout my studies I have found the word 'service' quoted at the top of the list of spiritual priorities.

Baba also says, "Mere formal worship or mumbling of hymns or mechanical routine performance of ritual, cannot induce God to reside in your heart. Liberation lies not in mystic formulae or rosaries, but stepping out into action". Once again, service before worship.

Sai Baba does not encourage us to give up our own particular religion to follow him. All religions have the same goal the difference lies in the individual interpretation of Truth. In this connection he says, "There is only one religion, the Religion of Love; there is only one caste, the Caste of Humanity; there is only one language, the Language of the Heart."

In keeping with the above teachings, his emblem incorporates symbols representing each of the five main religions of the world. They are a) The Cross of Christianity, b) The AUM of Hinduism, c) The Chakra of Buddhism, d) The Crescent and Star of Islam, and e) The Fire of Zoroastricism (Parsees). I was told that at Christmas, 1993, there was an estimated quarter of a million people at the Ashram to celebrate the festival.

Sai Baba never touches money. Donations sent to the Ashram are used in service. There are primary schools, colleges, universities and hospitals in India, all under the umbrella of his love.

In November 1991 one of the most revolutionary hospitals in the world was opened in Prasanthi Nilayam, in the poverty stricken state of Andrah Pradesh. Wealthy Baba devotees from around the globe provided the finance and expertise necessary for the project. Some of the most advanced medical equipment available has been installed. A number of devotees from the West, with the required qualifications, have gone there to work for next to nothing, since all treatment is free.

That is the kind of service which Sai Baba inspires in his followers.

The basic tenets of his teachings become an integral part of the lives of all the children who attend his schools. The building of character is deemed to be the most important aim of the education system. The children are taught Truth, Service to the Community, Self Discipline and Reverence of their Elders. They are shown that all people of every faith throughout the world are their brothers and sisters, because the divine spark of God dwells within each one.

So much has been written about Sai Baba's miracles that it is difficult to know where to begin. His whole life is a miracle and has been since his childhood. It became apparent to his family that he was 'special' when he was very young. At the age of four he would give food to beggars and have to go without himself. He did not appear to suffer any ill effects from this and did not seem to need the food. There is a tamarind tree near Puttaparthi from which he materialized different varieties of fruit for his school friends. Sometimes the fruit was out of season or did not grow naturally in that area.

He not only materializes vibhuti but rings, pendants, statues and food. He is able to materialize anything that is required.

Two friends of mine, Jane and John, were at the Ashram on Christmas Day 1982. This is their description of what happened.

"We trooped into the vast Poornachandra Hall with a crowd of several thousands, including many Westerners. We were to hear Baba deliver one of his homilies or 'discourses'. It was also the 85th birthday of Professor Kasturi. This former academic, highly literate in several languages, has devoted his life to Baba since 1954. He has written a number of biographical volumes on the subject of the Avatar.

We soon learned that everyone expected Baba to show him some special sign of favour. He did, and very quickly.

Baba stood up at his lectern on the dais and there was a hush throughout the hall. With virtually no preliminaries he declared that it was an occasion for particular rejoicing.

He advanced on Professor Kasturi (who towered over him by at least a foot and a half) and executed what has been described as 'that heart stopping circle of the hand'. From our position on the floor of the hall we saw a sudden bright flash in the air below the circling palm. Baba's hand at once swooped down and grasped a thick gold chain of considerable length carrying a very large gold pendant, which appeared from – who knows where? He tossed it almost nonchalantly over the head of the astonished Kasturi who was overcome and fell weeping to his knees."

There is no question of Sai Baba being a conjuror or a charlatan. If trickery had been involved it would have been uncovered many years ago. These materializations are not isolated, carefully orchestrated incidents.

He is what is known as omnipresent. If a soul in grave danger calls out to him he is able to project himself to their aid. He has been known to put 'life' back into a physical body, when death has occurred two days earlier.

Mediums who are able to see the human Aura, testify that Sai Baba's aura is pink and stretches to the horizon.

Baba says, without any hint of egotism, that nobody with human consciousness can understand who he is and that it is useless to try; one can only experience him.

He has said that it is beyond the capabilities of any number of scientists with any type of equipment to analyse him.

Do not dismiss what you have just read as mere fairy tales. Look into it for yourself. There are many, many books available covering every aspect of his life and teachings. They include, *The Embodiment of Love*, by Peggy Mason and Ron Laing, *The Ultimate Experience*, by Phyllis Krystal, *My Baba and I*, by Dr. John Hislop, S*ai Baba, the Holy Man and the Psychiatrist*, by Dr. Samuel Sandweiss, to name but a few.

## CHAPTER TWENTY-FIVE

On 5th January, 1993, I flew out from Heathrow Airport with thirteen other pilgrims bound for Bombay, en route to Puttaparthi. Although I had known about Sai Baba for fifteen years and had read many books about him, I did not consider myself a devotee. However, my spirit friends obviously wanted me to be able to experience him at first hand, and circumstances were arranged to allow me to do so. I even had two wins in the December Premium Bond draw, providing me with £150 towards my expenses.

January is supposed to be one of the cooler months in India, but I did not see a spot of rain in three weeks and the temperature was seldom below 85 degrees.

As I think back over my visit, the experience comes under two distinct headings – physical and spiritual. For the benefit of anyone who might be inspired to make the journey I shall begin by giving a fair 'warts and all' description of what the pilgrimage entails.

This trip is not for the faint-hearted. If you are not prepared for privation, do not consider making the journey.

On reaching Bombay it is necessary to cross the city to the Domestic Airport, in order to fly on to Bangalore – having run the gauntlet of about a hundred Indian porters all wanting to grab one's luggage in order to earn a few rupees. The decrepit bus organized for the transfer of passengers is about forty years old and of uncertain origin.

The air flight from Bombay to Bangalore takes just over an hour. Then one must repeat the business of fighting off dozens of porters and taxi drivers, all plying their trade. It is necessary to stay overnight in a hotel since the journey to Puttaparthi takes a further three hours by taxi.

The ride, in a 1950's vintage taxi, gives one the opportunity to see what rural life in Southern India is really like. Although I had travelled widely in Asia before, I had never seen poverty on the vast scale which I saw during my visit to this area of the sub-Continent. The way of life is biblical in its primitiveness.

Bullock carts are in use everywhere. Taxis are almost the only cars on the roads together with ancient trucks and lorries. In Bangalore scooters are the favourite mode of transport and sari-clad women are happy to ride pillion, side-saddle, carrying a child, with no crash helmet.

Horns wear out much more quickly than brakes in India. Drivers have their hand on the horn continuously warning people, cows, dogs, goats, monkeys and slower vehicles to make room for them. Roads are not wide and there is little space for passing.

The soil in that part of India is red and rocky. Crops of vegetables are grown and occasionally one sees a splash of bright green amongst the cultivated fields. I was told that it is mulberry leaves for feeding the silk worms which provide the famous Indian silk.

When asked to describe the Ashram I usually say it is like a primitive Holiday Camp, with no swimming pool, no alcohol and strict discipline.

It covers a huge area and consists of canteens, accommodation blocks for fifteen thousand people, a huge hall, called the Poonachandra, where Sai Baba gives his discourses, administration offices, shops and a museum. In the centre is the Mandir or temple. The Mandir is surrounded by a huge walled – in compound where 'darshan' is held twice daily. Footwear is forbidden in this area and there are piles of flip-flops etc along the pathways leading to it. Discarding footwear is also the custom when entering the canteen, the book shop or any administrative building.

No one wears western style dress at the Ashram, so it is advisable to take advantage of the stop over in Bangalore to kit oneself out in readiness. The majority of western women opt for the colourful Punjabi suits, consisting of baggy pants and knee length dress tops. Older ladies often prefer to wear long, loose Kaftans, while some brave souls sally forth in a sari. Personally, I did not venture out in a sari until almost the end of my stay, and even though I was well pinned, I was still uneasy about the whole lot collapsing around my feet. All women must wear a wide scarf or shawl around their arms and shoulders. On the last night I decided to go to the canteen without mine and strangely enough, after three weeks constant wear, I felt quite undressed without it.

The men wear loose, white baggy trousers and long white overshirts.

Strict segregation of the sexes is observed everywhere inside the Ashram gates. The Darshan area is carefully divided while there are separate canteens for men and women. Even the row of shops, which are like open fronted garages, have separate serving hatches for the two sexes. The thinking behind these rules is to cut out earthly distractions for the young devotees and to keep their minds on the spiritual pathway.

On arrival I think what took me most by surprise was the vast numbers of people there. Almost every nation on earth was represented – even the newly-formed Croatia. Naturally people from all over India were there in their thousands and it is still a mystery to me where they all slept. So, although everything one requires is available within the Ashram, there are always many other people in front of you with the same idea. The average time to cash a travellers' cheque was two hours and the Post Office was forever running out of stamps!

Living conditions, by Western standards, are appalling, but one has to keep in mind that the visit is a spiritual pilgrimage, not a sunshine holiday.

There are many enormous hanger-like buildings, known as the 'sheds', which house about 250 people each. The floors are marked off like a car park, and occupants curtain off their own little space with saris, towels etc. Mattresses may be bought quite cheaply in Puttaparthi village, which is right outside the walls of the Ashram and bedsteads are for hire. Organizing these basic requirements takes a great deal of time and energy when one first arrives, especially when the temperature is in the high eighties. In the large accommodation blocks, some of which are built in the round with a central courtyard, there are bare concrete rooms for four people with toilet and washing facilities (when they are working!), but no furniture.

The first few days are definitely a struggle for survival, but once one gets to know the 'ropes' and routine, things become a little easier. There is a great deal of sickness in the form of colds, coughs and diarrhoea. Vigilance must be the watchword with regard to eating and drinking. It is essential to have a high fluid intake but tap water must never be used in India, even for cleaning ones teeth. I discovered a water purifier in the canteen where bottles could be filled to take back to ones accommodation.

Since the numbers of devotees arriving from the Western World increases daily, there is now a special canteen run by and for Westerners. All food is vegetarian and one can live adequately on the equivalent £1 or less per day.

My day at the Ashram usually began around 5.00 a.m. when I got up ready for Darshan. Some people were up at 3.30 a.m. in order to take part in a special service held in the Temple, known as *Omkar*. This service is followed by the singing of bhajans (devotional songs, to the glory of God) in procession around the Ashram.

Although Sai Baba did not appear before 6.45 a.m., it was necessary to begin queuing by 5.30 a.m. to stand any chance of getting into the Darshan area. Many Indian men and women, known as Seva Dals, organize the day to day activities. Hundreds of them are on duty shepherding the thousands of people who want to be able to catch a glimpse of Sai Baba. It is a mammoth task, but with some of them I felt the little bit of power had gone to their heads, and I referred to them as the 'Gestapo'!

*Darshan at Brindavan (Whitefields). Sai Baba surrounded by his devotees.*

Everyone must sit on the floor at Darshan and I took a small seat with a back but no legs. The Seva Dals are continually telling everyone to move up closer to allow more people in at the back. After a few days of pushing and shoving I realized that sitting on the ground, crossed legged for about two hours was not for me, at over sixty years of age. I found that I was just wishing it would all be over so that I could stand up – and that wasn't what I had travelled half way round the world to experience. Once I got to know the 'ropes' I would queue up with the patients, who needed to sit on chairs and then slip round with my little seat and sit on a raised step where I had a view of Baba over everyone else's head.

The quietness of this huge gathering of people is quite extraordinary. Sometimes the numbers would be swelled by the students from his schools and colleges. They would attend morning Darshan in the same way our school children attend morning Assembly. The behaviour of these children was impeccable, even the very youngest.

Indian music played through a loudspeaker heralds the arrival of Sai Baba. The atmosphere is electric with all eyes straining for a glimpse of the orange-clad figure. The children in the front hold up platters of sweets for Baba to pick up and spray into the crowd. These were considered especially blessed because Baba had held them. Devotees in the front would try to persuade him to accept letters from them as he passed by. One very noticeable thing about Sai Baba is that he seems to smoothly glide along when he walks and never hurries.

Most Westerners arrive in groups and each group wears its own special coloured scarf. While he is walking around he will sometimes ask a male devotee how many are with him. He will then indicate that the group should go to the Mandir for a private meeting at the conclusion of Darshan. Although scattered throughout the compound the group is easily identified amongst the many thousands by their distinctive scarves.

When one reads the many books written by Sai Baba's devotees, a private interview seems to be the natural course of events. That may have been so ten or twenty years ago but it is certainly not the case now. A private meeting must be looked upon as an incredible bonus. Although we were in India for three weeks, never missed a Darshan while he was in residence and even travelled over a hundred miles to Bangalore to be in his presence, we did not receive this honour. One just has to console oneself with the thought that those chosen must be in greater need.

Life inside the Ashram becomes so absorbing that the outside world ceases to exist. A Third World War could have broken out and we would have been oblivious of the fact.

## CHAPTER TWENTY-SIX

To recount spiritual experiences is a far more difficult task than narrating physical ones. Writing about emotions which were triggered off in the heat of colourful, vibrant, spiritual India becomes a mammoth undertaking beneath the dull, grey, bleak skies of an English winter's day. However, I shall do my best to describe these more abstract memories.

On the first morning while I was sitting on the ground in the Darshan compound, surrounded by literally thousands of other cramped women, I saw the dawn break over the Mandir. The building is carved in the Hindu tradition and painted pastel pink and blue. As I watched the sky turn from deepest purple to a pale cerise I became aware of tears streaming down my face. The sheer beauty of that first Indian dawn will remain in my memory for ever.

During the early days my emotions were very near the surface. I became very upset that no one appeared to care about the dogs and cats which lived in the Ashram. All the talk about Baba being the embodiment of Love and present in all living things, seemed to me to be empty words when I saw the state of the animals. Later, I realized there were a number of others like me who were concerned and helped in practical ways, such as feeding. However, the situation still leaves much to be desired. Somehow, one must leave Western standards behind when one touches down in India, difficult as it may be.

Before I left England I had asked my friend Brother John 'on the other side' if he had any advice for me, and the reply was, "No, you are a seasoned traveller, but Beware of Emotionalism." I soon realized to what he had been referring. The spiritual energy is incredibly strong but it affects people in different ways.

Many ardent devotees are happy to find an excuse for everything which happens to them at the Ashram. If they get a streaming cold or go down with dysentery they say it is Baba's way of using physical means to cleanse them spiritually. I do not fall into that category. However, he does say we should leave behind all our excess baggage when we go to visit him. By that he means our jealousies, hatreds, pride, egotism, material attachments – all those negative characteristics which will cloud our spiritual eyes and hamper our appreciation of what he has to offer. That of course is easier said than done, but I found out he sometimes provides the means for us to do this.

About four days after our arrival our group leader arranged for us to meet with a lovely English lady who has given up her comfortable life in England to work permanently for Sai Baba at the Ashram. She does a form of psychotherapy called 'Cutting the ties that Bind'. Although I had heard of the book with that title I had never enquired what it really meant. A psychotherapist and Sai Baba devotee named Phyllis Krystal had written the book to share with others the results of twenty years work in the psychotherapy field.

Briefly, the thinking behind the therapy is as follows. We are all influenced in our adult lives by what happened to us in childhood, during our developmental years. Our spiritual progress is hampered by these experiences and the deep scars which are still in our sub-conscious mind influence our present behaviour. 'Cutting the Ties' helps us to cast aside all these negative associations which we no longer need.

At the first session we were told to relax and meditate for a while in order to discover within ourselves from whose influence we needed to break away. I did not need to meditate as I knew I had carried around hatred of my stepmother for half a century. There were nine of us in the group and each one realized that we needed to cut a connection with someone.

The therapy began by visualizing oneself surrounded by a ring of golden light. When we were happy with that we were then told to create another golden ring which was just touching our own. Into that ring we had to call the person from whom we had to cut the tie. Once we could clearly see our two selves in the golden rings we then visualized a blue line of energy making a figure of eight around the adjoining circles.

Under normal conditions one should carry out this exercise four times a day for two weeks. However, the energies in the Ashram are such that the procedure is only necessary for three days. One is then ready to 'Cut the Tie'.

On the third day we again met with our therapist. We were told to make ourselves comfortable and begin with our visualization exercise. The next step was to decide for ourselves which part of our body was linked with the other person and to visualize the material form of the connection.

For many years I had carried around a knot of nerves in my solar plexus region and I knew exactly where the link was and what form it took. I went on to visualize a lump of wire wool, like a pan scrubber, which I pulled out of myself in a long strand. I looked at the pile and then saw myself throw the whole lot into a furnace and get rid of it for ever.

The therapist was gently leading us through the exercise and when we had disposed of the mental debris she told us to fill the gap with all the love which we had longed for all our lives, but never had. We were to see it pouring into us upwards from Mother Earth and downwards from Father Sun.

As I carried out her suggestions I could feel my emotions coming to the surface and then the dam burst. I wept uncontrollably for about ten minutes. If this had not happened to me I would not have believed that visualization could have such a dramatic effect.

Our therapist told us not to discuss our reactions between ourselves or with anyone else for three days, because the therapy was still working. We were also told to write a letter to the other person forgiving them for what they had done to us and asking forgiveness for our own behaviour. The letter had to be torn up in three days.

Before I began this therapy there had been nothing physically wrong with me. After it, my head streamed nonstop and likewise my lower regions. Three days later I tore up the letter and everything went back to normal.

That is how Baba helped me to rid myself of fifty years of hatred. Perhaps those who say Baba cleanses us spiritually by physical means are right after all!

## CHAPTER TWENTY-SEVEN

Before I left for India many friends, who knew all about Sai Baba, said they would be waiting eagerly to hear my assessment of him. They wanted confirmation 'straight from the horses mouth' that he is, who he says he is.

During my search for spiritual Truth I have always let my intellect cloud my spiritual understanding. Sai Baba makes a point of warning devotees about this, but I am the original doubting Thomasina. Throughout the world there are many devout Sai Baba devotees who will probably never see him in human form but are prepared to follow his teachings. I'm afraid I am not one of them. I always need proof.

Consequently, I sat at Darshan twice a day, looking at him and expecting some wonderful revelation. Nothing happened. Although I was surrounded by thousands of ardent devotees I still only knew him in my head, from what I had read about him, and not in my heart.

I saw him materialize vibhuti on several occasions. One morning he made a swift circular movement with his hand and produced a golden chain holding a medallion, which he put over the head of a little boy aged about seven. At the back of my mind I was still wondering what I was going to say to the people 'back home'.

All the time I was allowing my intellect to obstruct my inner spiritual powers of recognition. Sai Baba knew this and chose a very dramatic way in which to prove to me that he is omnipresent. I now know that prayers are answered and when he says, "Why fear when I am here", he means it.

The story begins at the Ashram on Monday, 19th January. Sai Baba had left the previous Saturday and several of us had followed him to Bangalore in order to attend Darshan at Brindavan on the Sunday morning. We returned to Puttaparthi the same afternoon, as Baba was going on to Madras for a few days. It is said that he sometimes leaves the Ashram in order to disperse the enormous crowds which build up.

At about 9.15 a.m. on the Monday morning I was lying on my bed (no chairs) reading a book about Sai Baba, when I decided to walk round the Ashram and take a few photographs with my camera. When Baba is in residence there are rules about where one may or may not use photographic equipment.

I was standing by the Ashram gate which leads into Puttaparthi village. This village is a microcosm of all India. Beggars, young and old are everywhere, with their hands out. The shops are just open-fronted shanties and the streets are full of goats, donkeys, bullock carts and women sitting on the ground with baskets of produce for sale. The contrast as one steps back into the orderliness of the Ashram is astonishing. There are male Seva Dals always on duty vetting who comes through the gates.

As I stood taking a few snaps I was approached by an Indian gentleman and his family, who were just leaving the Ashram. He introduced himself as Mr. Rao and said he was a school teacher. He asked to have a look at my camera and I offered to take some photographs of his family. Cameras are luxuries which few Indian families can afford. As we were exchanging our names and addresses he said, "We are going to the Temple at Tirupathi". When I looked blank he went on, "It is the most famous Temple in India – *God is there*. Come with us."

"I couldn't do that", I protested, but he kept on trying to persuade me to change my mind.

Then he asked if I had any pens which he could give to his pupils. Strangely enough wherever you go in India, school children ask for pens. Presumably Indian ones must be of poor quality. I had been told about this before I left England so I bought a number of biros which I could distribute. I told him I would go back to my room and get them. Still he kept insisting that I should accompany his family on the bus to Tirupathi. I asked how far it was and he told me 200 kilometres. He said there was overnight accommodation there, the same as at the Ashram, and I could travel back to Puttaparthi the following day.

About half an hour before this incident I had been reading an anecdote about a lady who was expecting Sai Baba for a meal when a dog appeared at the door. She shooed it away. Sai Baba did not arrive for the meal and at a later date he said, "I came but you sent me away". He was illustrating that he is present in all living things. This story was very fresh in my mind and when one is on a spiritual 'high', as one is at the Ashram, one looks for hidden meanings in all situations. I began to wonder if Baba was setting this up for me. Perhaps there was something at the Temple at Tirupathi which he wanted me to experience and write about. (I had religiously taken my manuscript to Darshan every day and held it up for his blessing).

The idea of travelling on an Indian bus for 200 kilometres was a daunting prospect but I made a quick calculation in my head and realized we would arrive in the early afternoon. There would be plenty of time to see the Temple. So after more cogitating I finally agreed to go. Mr. Rao wrote his name and address and the name of our destination for my room mates while I gathered together a few overnight things. Off we went.

We made our way through the village to the bus station and there was to be about a twenty minute wait before departure. I decided to hurry down to the photography shop and get a new film put in my camera. During my absence Mr. Rao had bought tickets for his family, (wife, mother-in-law, three children and his younger brother). He asked for my fare money and I boarded the bus with the family, while he went to purchase my ticket. Indian buses are like nothing you have ever seen in England unless it is on a hippie commune!

The family sat half way down the bus, but I saw an open window at the back and decided that was the place for me. It was sweltering hot. Mr. Rao came back with my ticket, (it cost 66 rupees, about £1.40p) and said my seat was number 39. I looked up and discovered that I had chosen to sit in seat number 39. The thought, could that just be a coincidence, flashed through my mind. I began to think that this journey was 'meant'.

We left Puttaparthi at 10.15 a.m. and after travelling over bumpy roads for half an hour a gentleman, aged about thirty, got on and sat next to me. When he spoke I was amazed at his cultured command of English. It was so different from Mr. Rao's Indian-type English. He told me he was a Civil Servant working in the tax department. He hoped to go to England soon to study our taxation methods. We had been travelling through the most poverty-stricken countryside it is possible to see anywhere on earth, and I said to him, "Who pays taxes in India? I have never seen such poverty." He replied, "For every hundred people in the population, only seven pay taxes." Those statistics speak for themselves!

At about twelve o'clock we stopped at a bus station in a small town. The heat was unbearable and Mr. Rao suggested I should get off the bus and have a cold drink. I was very careful to consume only bottled drinks throughout this whole trip. As I stood thankfully sucking up my lemonade I realized a crowd had gathered. I don't think some of them had ever seen a white woman before and you don't see many people of my ample proportions in India. I felt like a specimen in a zoo! Mrs. Rao showed me to the first of many toilets which I encountered for which I can find no words in the English language to describe!

On returning to the bus I overheard Mr. Rao and the civil servant conversing, and I heard 7.30 p.m. mentioned. I was horrified to learn that we would not be arriving in the early afternoon, but in the evening. The distance was not 200 kilometres but 340. It was too late to do anything about my predicament. One cannot get off a bus in the middle of the barren Indian countryside and wait for the next bus back. Too late I realized how foolish and impetuous I had been. Every minute took me further away from everything which was familiar to me, and every uncomfortable mile would have to be retravelled on the return journey. My faith in Mr. Rao evaporated rapidly.

I learned from the gentleman next to me that the Temple which I was to visit was not in Tirupathi, but an hour's taxi ride up into the hills. He also told me what an important temple it is and he also said, "God is there."

Hour after relentless hour we bounced our way across central India. I scarcely ate or drank anything all day for fear of the dreaded Delhi belly. Every so often we would stop in small settlements to allow more and more peasants to board the bus. There was only one passenger who was of the educated class and he was sitting next to me. Coincidence?

A situation which is quite easy to handle during daylight hours becomes a different proposition once night begins to fall, which it did soon after six o'clock. I remember looking out of the bus window up into the sky and seeing the evening star smiling down at me. I recalled how I would gaze up at this star at home while walking my dogs and pondering the wonders of the Universe. This time I was more concerned with survival than the unexplained mysteries of Space.

I was managing to keep my rising panic in check when a lorry came past from the opposite direction and banged the side of the bus, exactly where I was sitting. I was petrified, expecting to have to get out of the bus into the pitch darkness with a crowd of strangers. My money belt contained more in cash and travellers cheques than most of them had seen in their entire lives. I just sat there silently screaming out to Sai Baba to please help me.

After much discussion and inspection of the damage by the light of oil lamps, the decision was made to continue our journey. As the bus began to move the civil servant leaned over and said to me, "Don't be scared – you know Sai Baba says, Why fear when l am here", convincing me that the young man was put next to me by Baba. "I've been telling myself that for hours", I gasped, "but it is becoming more and more difficult". He said he would give me his phone number in case I needed help. It was a kind gesture, but knowing what public services are like in India the offer did nothing to allay my fears.

The road got worse, if that was possible and we were literally bouncing up in the air. I continued to call out frantically to Sai Baba to send someone else to help me, as I had totally lost faith in Mr. Rao.

*Sudha and Rani with Mr. Rao and his brother.*

At about 7.30 p.m. we drew into the blackness of Tirupathi Bus Station. By this time I was inwardly quaking, wondering where on earth I was going to spend the night. The bus was very crowded and I was the last to get off. As I shakily climbed down the steps of the bus into the darkness, two arms were suddenly thrown tightly around me and I heard a beautiful voice in impeccable English saying, "Do not be scared, Mama, Sai Baba is with us. He will take care of us".

I peered down into the two most radiant, shining eyes I have ever seen in my life. They were looking up out of the face of a young Nepalese woman, who was no more that 4 feet 10 inches in height. I shall remember that moment for all eternity.

There was the usual milling crowd of people wanting to carry ones luggage and I heard Mr. Rao saying somewhere in the darkness, "What are you scared about?" I realized that the Civil Servant must have said as he got off the bus, "The English lady is very frightened."

My Nepalese friend continued to hold me in a vice like grip and said, "Come to a Hotel with us, my sister is just seeing to the luggage." In that moment I 'knew' that this was the answer to my prayers and I was going to stay with these two young Nepalese women. I told Mr. Rao that I would not be accompanying him and his family.

We picked our way through the darkness, with my friend still gripping my hand and giving me her strength. Within half an hour the two sisters had negotiated a room for the three of us and we were sitting drinking coffee and telling each other our life stories. It was a very low grade hotel even by Indian standards, but we did not mind so long as we were together. The price doubled when they saw my European features, but even so the night's lodging only cost us the equivalent of £1 each.

I learnt that they were both school teachers, studying for their Masters degrees. They came from a highly religious, cultured, Hindu family belonging to the Brahmin caste, and had been speaking English as a second language since childhood. The whole family were devotees of Sai Baba. They had been staying at the Ashram and had decided to visit the temple at Tirupathi before catching the train home from Bangalore. I had not noticed them amongst the crowds on the bus because they were sitting at the front. One of the sisters told me that during her daily meditation she always asks to be of service to Sai Baba. She was certainly used by him on that occasion, for which I shall be eternally grateful.

We did not sleep much that night because there was so much noise in the hotel, and we were up very early. Mr. Rao had arranged to pick us up the next morning at 7 o'clock. We would have preferred to have gone on our own, but he arrived on time and we all travelled in the same taxi.

The contrast to the barren landscape of the previous day was extraordinary. We drove up through an area of green wooded Forestry Commission land for about an hour.

The temple was not in the least what I had expected. It covered a huge area and was like a large village. We had to leave our shoes in the taxi, (fortunately I was wearing socks) and start walking. Once more the crowds were incredible. I glimpsed the golden roof of the actual temple from a distance, but that was as near as I got to it. It was going to take three or four hours of queuing in the boiling hot sun to go inside. So, if God was there, I certainly didn't come across him. I had seen him the night before in those radiant eyes which had looked up at me, in my time of distress.

All I wanted to do was get away from the crowds, and so did my friends. Mr. Rao was still insisting that he wanted to show us his temple, but we would have none of it, and made our way back to the taxi. On the way we passed a huge place like a swimming pool, with steps all round leading down into the water, where people were taking ritual baths before entering the temple.

The ride back down the sixty two hair pin bends into Tirupathi town, in a thirty year old taxi, was not a pleasant experience. As the only driver amongst the passengers, I was also the only person to be concerned when the taxi driver had to stop and put oil in his brakes and water in the radiator!

We were dropped off at the Coach Station, as we had decided to travel straight on to Bangalore. I could not have faced another nine hour journey back to Puttaparthi in a local bus, alone. Fortunately a coach was leaving in the early afternoon and we were able to book seats. It could not have been more different from the vehicle of the previous day. It was brand new, with reclining seats and a video.

It was about a five hour journey to Bangalore and once more we arrived in the dark. However, this time we were in a busy city, and although my friends were not familiar with it, I soon had us all in a small auto-taxi en route to the hotel, which I had stayed in on two previous occasions. The traffic was horrendous, but after what I had been through during the past thirty six hours I was impervious to it. Unfortunately it was a case of 'No room at the Inn', and the Manager told me that all the hotels in Bangalore were full. Another hurdle to overcome! The taxi driver said he knew of another hotel, so off we went again. Still no luck. Back into the chaotic traffic once more and on to another hotel. I suggested that we all start praying!

It was third time lucky and we found a room for the three of us. As I was signing the register, I looked up, and there was a huge photograph of Sai Baba looking down at me. He had his finger up, as much as to say, 'I told you not to worry.'

We had a good meal followed by a welcome night's sleep. In the morning I arranged a taxi to take me back to Puttaparthi. When it came to parting from my two friends we were all feeling very emotional. Although we had known each other for less that forty-eight hours there was a tremendous bond between us. I feel we shall meet again one day. Perhaps we had been together in previous lives – who knows?

During my three hour taxi ride back to the Ashram, I was conscious of what I can only describe as a feeling of sheer *bliss* inside me. I have never had the feeling before. I sat there glowing with something akin to complete ecstasy. I did not want the journey to end. Furthermore I did not want to share the experience straight away. It is impossible to really explain a spiritual experience to anyone else, because it is such a personal thing – only meant for the one concerned. No one else can really understand the impact of it, and my advice is to keep it close to you, unless you can be sure that the other person can empathise with the situation.

Somewhere deep inside me I knew that Sai Baba had revealed himself to me and at last I knew him in my heart and not just in my head.

## CHAPTER TWENTY-EIGHT

I began my story by quoting the words spoken to me by a medium whom I had never previously met. That was only one event which indicated to me that spirit friends were influencing my work.

In the first few months of writing, on at least four occasions, the most unlikely people said to me, "I came across this book and thought you might be interested in it." Each time there was something of great value which helped me to plan the form the book should take.

Each day I would sit on my own in the Sanctuary, scribbling away, thinking, "Well, they've told me it's going to be published, but how? I don't know any writers and I certainly don't have the faintest idea how to get a book published."

One day, a young woman brought her mother to see us for healing. We could tell by the way she spoke that she was a 'free thinker', and on the same spiritual wavelength as ourselves. Out of the blue, I handed her my latest chapter and said, "Would you read this while we treat your mother, and tell me what you think?" I'm still amazed that I said this to a stranger, even though I now realize it was all part of the plan. When she read it she said, "It's funny you should ask me this because I spend all my time writing. There is a writers' seminar not far from here on Saturday, and a writers' group meets every Wednesday in the next village."

Within half an hour I had signed up for the seminar and joined the writers' group. Thus, I was put in touch with people who are interested in writing and know all about publishers and publishing. Once again this could be put down to coincidence, but I 'know' it was planned. The spirit world want this book to be published and that was their way of setting the wheels in motion.

There were even more amazing arrangements being made which even now I marvel at.

During the Spring and Summer of 1992, I sent my manuscript to a number of publishers, but each time the reply was the same. They found the content interesting, but in this time of recession could not become involved with a book which had such a limited appeal to the buying public. One gentleman suggested that he could possibly consider it under a cost sharing scheme. This pathway was quite unacceptable since it would have entailed risking several thousands of pounds and put my present standard of living in jeopardy. I had to comfort myself with the knowledge that even Frederick Forsyth received many rejection slips before his first book was published.

Eventually in November, 1992, during one of our circle meetings, I asked Brother John whether I should abandon thoughts of publication until after my forthcoming visit to India the following January. The reply was that the book was not yet complete and there would be other experiences to write about.

I certainly did have plenty to relate on my return and several months later I felt the book was complete and sent it off to another publisher. A two month wait for an acknowledgement resulted in another rejection. I was at a loss to know what my next move should be.

I was still attending the writers group and there was always much discussion about outlets for our literary works. Popular magazines which paid money for published letters were mentioned and on one red-letter day I received £5 in payment for one of my efforts. Until it was brought to my attention in this way I had never even heard of this publication. I noticed that this particular magazine specializes in competitions, and since I had taken up 'comping' as a hobby decided to buy it regularly.

Six weeks later, on 10th July, the unbelievable happened.

I WON A CAR!

My excitement knew no bounds and I even rang friends in Australia to pass on the amazing news.

Once things had quietened down, at the back of my mind was the niggling question, "Why me"? The odds against this happening, judging by the circulation figures, must be a million to one. Since we already had two vehicles I had every intention of selling it and enjoying the proceeds.

A few days after my husband and I had been to London for the presentation we held our regular meeting with our Group 'on the other side'. During our time for questions I mentioned my disappointment regarding non-publication of the book. The reply was, *"Why don't you publish it privately. Now you have the money?"* I said that because it had been turned down so many times I felt it was not good enough. They replied, *"That is not so. Publishers are only interested in profit. When it is difficult to sell books even Archer is left on the shelf."* I asked if Jeffrey

*Mike and I enjoying ourselves at the presentation of the car.*

Archer had been inspired by spirit and the reply was, *"Not in the same way that you have been."* I realised then that I had been looking at it from the wrong angle and their remarks about profit motive were quite correct.

"So that's why I won the car!", I exclaimed. *"Of course. But beware of sharks,"* was the reply. It is well-known in literary circles that there are some very unscrupulous vanity publishers (as they are called). So I even received a warning from them regarding the pitfalls of private publishing.

Twelve months before I could not possibly have contemplated spending several thousands of pounds in this manner. All the way through I had been assured that everything would fall into place when the time was right. When I calculated the total cost including publishing, buying a word processor, reams and reams of paper etc. I would say that give or take a few pounds the whole project has been paid for by the money I received in payment for the car.

Once again no doubt the sceptics would scoff at the mere idea that it was planned in this way, but those of us who understand the workings of the spirit world *know*.

E. G. Bulwer-Lytton said, "The pen is mightier than the sword", and I hope this will be so in my case.

If just a few young people read and understand that they are responsible for their own behaviour, and realize there is a meaning behind everyone's life, then my work will not have been in vain.

Hopefully I have managed to sow a handful of seeds in a few fertile minds. Perhaps the owners of those minds will stand back and really see what suffering is being perpetrated throughout the world in the name of man-made religions and do something about it in the years to come.

The road to spiritual understanding is not an easy one. No other person will have the same experiences as myself. We are all at different stages in our evolvement and have different paths to follow.

However, I can assure everyone that their journey will be as equally exciting and rewarding as mine has been once they are committed to searching for the real Truth.

Everything chronicled here is the Truth as I experienced and perceived it. The only deviation has been to alter names, to preserve anonimity. I'm sure those concerned will recognise themselves under a different title.

Having come across every kind of fear, bigotry, indifference and indoctrination during our search, my husband and I would like to leave you with the following ancient prayer, of unknown origin.

> *From the Laziness that is content with Half Truth,*
> *From the Cowardice that shrinks from New Truth,*
> *And from the Arrogance that feels it knows All Truth,*
> *Oh, God of Truth deliver us!*

PAX VOBISCUM.

# BIBLIOGRAPHY AND SUGGESTED FURTHER READING

*The Healing Touch* by M. H. Tester.
*God is My Witness* by E. Fricker.
*I Fly Out with Bright Colours* by Allegra Taylor.
*The Wise Virgin* by Annie Wilson.
*Let the Petals Fall* by Margaret, Countess of Wraxall.
*My Research into the Unknown* by Gladys Archer.
*Science of the Gods* by David Ash and Peter Hewitt.
*Other Worlds* by Paul Davies.
*The Story of Helen Duncan* by Alan Crossley.
*Arigo – Surgeon of the Rusty Knife* by John Fuller.
*Edgar Cayce – Man of Miracles* by Joseph Millard.
*Wonder Healers of the Philippines* by Harold Sherman.
*The History of Christianity* by Michael Roll.
*The Suppression of Knowledge* by Michael Roll.
*The Physicists and Nationalists Case for Survival after Death of the Physical Body* by Michael Roll.
*Cutting the Ties That Bind* by Phyllis Krystal.
*The Living Image* by Coral Polge.
*Look Beyond Today* by Rosemary Brown.
*Mediums and their Work* by Linda Williamson.
*Voices in my Ear* by Doris Stokes.
*Woman of Spirit* by Doris Collins.
*Out on a Limb* by Shirley Maclaine.
*Dancing in the Light* by Shirley Maclaine.
*The Seed of Truth – Teachings of Silver Birch*,
*A Voice in the Wilderness – Teachings from Silver Birch.*
*When Your Child Dies* by Sylvia Barbanell.
*When Your Animal Dies* by Sylvia Barbanell.
*The Bewildered Man's Guide to Death* by M. H. Tester.
*Beyond the Spectrum* by Cyril Permutt.
*The Mediumship of Jack Webber* by Harry Edwards.
*Harry Edwards – Life Story of a Great Healer* by Ramus Branch.
*Second Time Around* by E. Ryall.
*The Embodiment of Love* by Peggy Mason and Ron Laing.
*Sai Baba and the Psychiatrist* by Samuel Sandweiss.
*My Baba and I* by Dr. John Hislop.
*The Ultimate Experience* by Phyllis Krystal. (Sai Baba).

*Living Divinity (Sai Baba)* by Shakuntala Baiu.
Sai Baba Avatar by Howard Murphet.
*Life Between Life* by Dr. Joel L. Witton.
*The History of Spiritualism* by Sir Arthur Donan Doyle.

## USEFUL ADDRESSES

*Anyone wishing to know the name and address of a reputable spiritual healer in their area should contact:-*

The National Federation of Spiritual Healers,
Old Manor Farm Studio
Church Street
Sunbury on Thames
Middlesex
TW16 6RG
Tell. 0937 68164

*Reputable Spiritualist Mediums are at work every day at:-*

The Spiritualist Association of Great Britain
38 Belgrave Square
London SW1
Tel. 071 235 3351

*Recommended International Medium:-*

Paula Wood
15 Bulrush Close
Swan Waters
St. Mellons
Cardiff
Tel. 0222 797682

*Courses on every aspect of Spiritual Matters are held at:-*

The Arthur Findlay College
Stansted Hall
Mountfitchet
Stansted
Essex
Tel. 0279 813686